BLOG BLAZERS

40 TOP BLOGGERS SHARE THEIR SECRETS

to Creating a High-Profile, High-Traffic, and High-Profit Blog!

STEPHANE GRENIER

Levac Publishing House
Suite 206 – 5929L Jeanne D'Arc Blvd.
Ottawa, Ontario
Canada
K1C 7K2

Author: Stephane Grenier.
ISBN: 978-0-9810852-0-3
BlogBlazers.com

Table of Contents

Acknowledgements

Firstly I'd like to thank all my friends and family who made this book possible, which is a lot of people. I know I will miss some, but I'd really like to single out my wife whom without her support and editing, this book never would have made it to print.

Another person I'd like to thank is my friend Sam. He was gracious enough to offer his time to do a first edit of the book, before it was even completed. His edits really helped. Thank you Sam.

And without a doubt, a great big thank you goes to everyone who agreed to participate in this book and take the time to be interviewed. Without you this book wouldn't even exist. Thank you

Stephane Grenier
September 2008

Preface

The idea to write this book came to me almost half a year before I actually sat down to write it. It came to me when I was one of two main speakers at a seminar during the summer of 2007 on how to make money on the internet. My particular presentation was on how to increase a website's traffic through both free and paid methods.

As I was preparing for the presentation I thought this same material would make a great book if re-written in book format. I had a lot to share on how to increase a website's traffic. Having successfully founded my own company LandlordMax Software Inc. in 2003, and started my own personal blog (FollowSteph.com) in 2005, I already knew what was involved in building traffic for websites. Today LandlordMax gets about 300,000 unique visitors a year (which is great for a niche software market) and FollowSteph.com is getting about 500,000 unique visitors a year.

So I decided that after finishing the seminar I would sit down and write the book. I wrote about my idea in May of 2007 on my blog (http://www.followsteph.com/2007/05/02/marketing-and-sales-for-small-online-businesses/), even going so far as summarizing all the chapters of the book.

With the idea much more concrete, and a detailed plan of attack, I set off to write the book. I got a full three chapters completed, even lining up a few mini interviews (case studies). Then I realized that although this was a great idea, and I will eventually go back to finishing this book, I was very much more active on the blogging side of things. Blogging has now become my main source of marketing and advertising for LandlordMax.

How so? My blog FollowSteph.com is the main source of traffic and sales to LandlordMax after the search engines! The blog, which was started two years after LandlordMax was founded, gets more traffic than LandlordMax itself. This is not surprising, you only go back to a corporate website when you need something whereas a blog is a continual source of information.

I basically came to the realization that if someone could blog successfully, they would be more effective in generating traffic to their company than by directly marketing and advertising it. That's what happened to me.

Of course it's never that simple. You can create a blog that gets a lot of traffic but doesn't convert. The reality is that if you want it to convert it has to be related to your business, and you need to be real. With FollowSteph I talk about what it takes to run a small business. I talk about our successes AND our failures. I'm honest. I explain who we are. I explain why and how we do things. I give people a behind the scenes look at me and my business. Many people appreciate this, it personalizes the company. They might not always agree with our decisions, but at least they understand why. And so far, it's been a very positive and rewarding experience. I wouldn't have it any other way.

Evidently you can't just talk about yourself. Although I frequently talk about LandlordMax, I also give out valuable information to my readers. I give them tips on how to run their businesses. I talk about marketing. I talk about success. I talk about software development. I talk about customer service. Basically anything we have to deal with on a day to day basis.

Getting back to my original point, after I realized that blogging was my most successful traffic building effort, I started to think what and how I could write about it. I didn't want to be another "How to blog" book, or ebook. I wanted to be different. I wanted to create something more. Then I bought a copy of the book "Founders at Work". It's a book written by Jessica Livingston where she interviews many great company founders about their experiences and knowledge in starting a company. I was so impressed with the book that as soon as I was done I recommended it on my blog (http://www.followsteph.com/2007/09/09/founders-at-work/). It's a great book, I can't say enough about it!

And this is when the idea for the book you're about to start reading today came to me. I thought that instead of just me sharing what I've learned, I'd interview the most prominent bloggers out there already succeeding. I'd ask them the same questions. See what they thought. How they differed in opinions. What was similar. What really worked for them. How they defined their success. And am I glad I did. As I was compiling the interviews I was still learning an incredible amount! These people are smart and they know what they are doing, so I'm listening. Even though I've been successful in my own ways, I still have much to learn from them.

All that lead to this book. I sent out many interview invitations and as you can see some great people responded. I hope you will learn as much from them as I did. And if you do, please don't hesitate to let us know. I'd love to hear about it, as I'm sure they would!

Introduction

Blogging is a fairly new concept, only as recently as 1999 was it accepted as a word in the dictionary. Webster defines a blog as "a Web site that contains an online personal journal with reflections, comments, and often hyperlinks provided by the writer". Blogging is the action of writing this content, and a blogger is the person doing the writing.

What's interesting is that the definition of blogging is very large. It's so large that if you ask people if they read blogs, they'll say no. Not because they don't read them, but because they don't realize what a blog is. The reality is that virtually everyone reads blogs. Blogs are prolific. They're everywhere. In fact, there are now 70 million blogs, growing at a rate of 1.4 blogs every second according to Technorati.com!

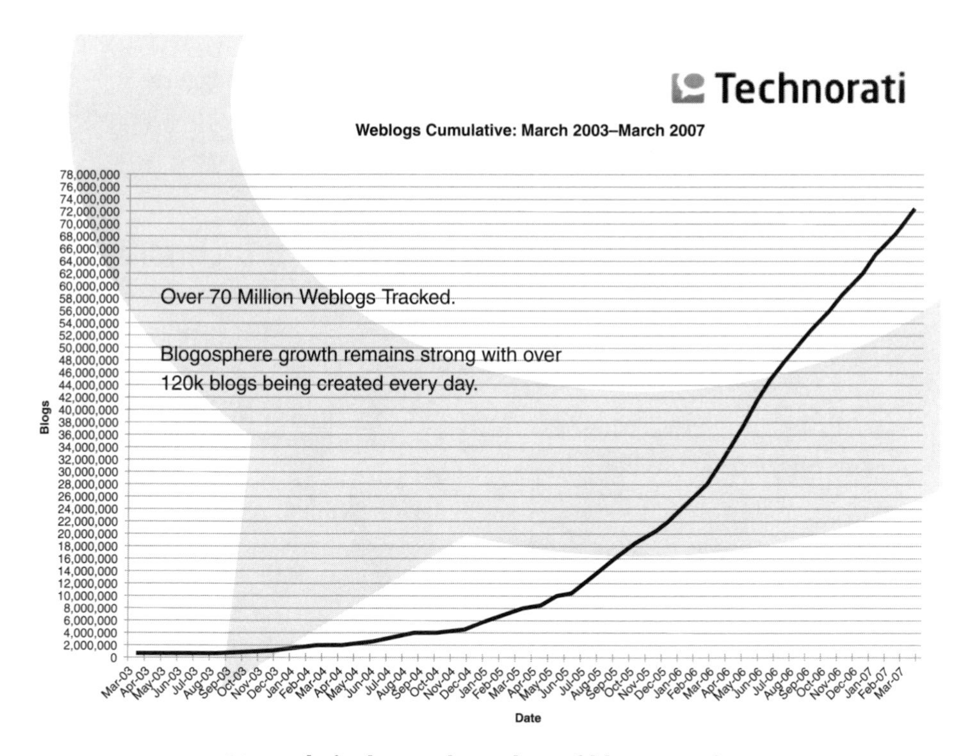

Not only is the total number of blogs growing, but the rate at which new blogs are created is also growing.

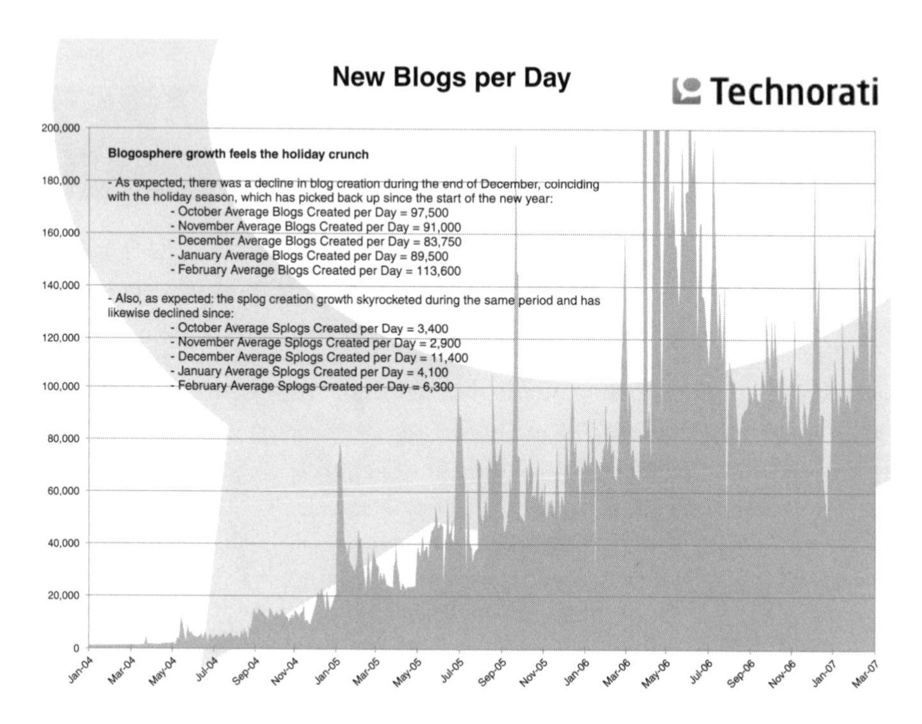

And if you think that wasn't enough, the combined bloggers are posting 1.4 million posts/day and growing.

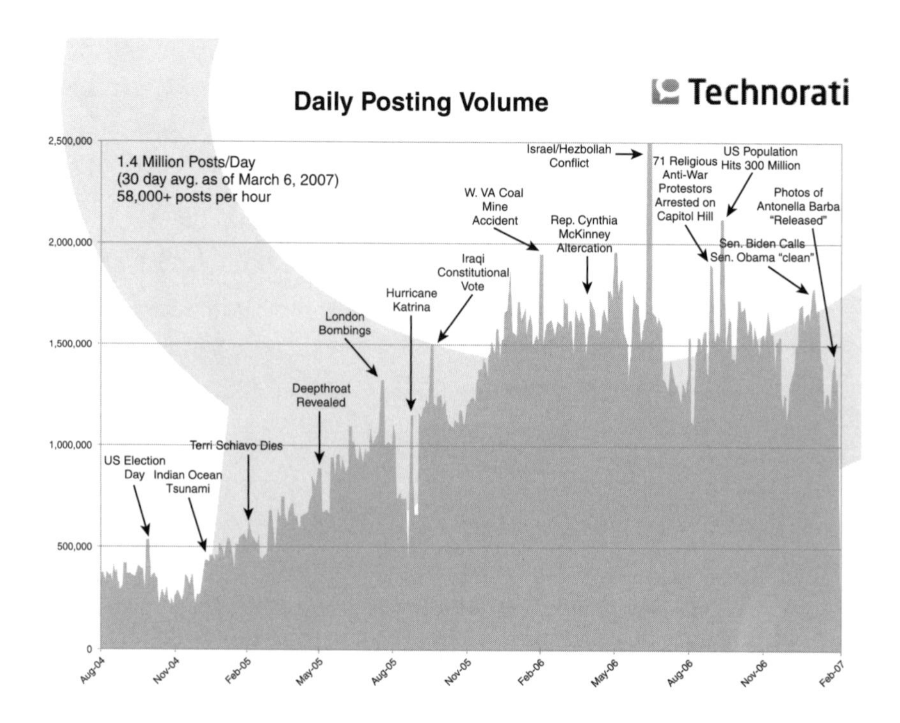

To summarize with some quick metrics, there are:

- 70 million weblogs
- About 120,000 new weblogs each day, or 1.4 new blogs every second
- 3,000-7,000 new splogs (splogs are fake or spam blogs with the sole objective to make money) created every day
- 1.5 million posts per day or 17 posts per second

You can find these and more great statistics from Technorati.com about blogging and bloggers at http://www.sifry.com/alerts/archives/000493.html.

The fact that there are so many blogs however doesn't mean that they're all good, or even decent. Most are pretty weak and die out within a few weeks to months (not counting splogs). The blogosphere is littered with dead blogs. This is mainly because the barrier to entry to start a blog is very low while the barrier to great success is very high. Because of this, many people try and start a new blog but drop their efforts within a short time.

The obvious question then is why blog? What are the benefits? Why are so many people blogging? Generally it comes down to a few small reasons. Right now, the most common reason is the perception that blogging can make you a lot of money with very little effort. That's far from the truth. Most of the very successful bloggers today that are making a lot of money have been blogging for years. To use one of my favorite sayings, "It took me 10 years to become an overnight success".

Then why do people do it? Why do they put in so much effort? Why do sports athletes train so hard when only a handful will succeed? Why do people move to Hollywood to become movies stars when the odds are ridiculously small? Because the benefits of success are worth it. That or they just really like to write (which is the case for many people).

But for most people, they have a specific goal they want to achieve. It can be a certain level of revenue, it can be a certain size of readership, it can be a certain level of expertise, and so on. In essence, they start a blog with a goal in mind and strive to achieve that goal.

The most common goal, at least from the media's perspective, is to start a blog to generate revenue directly from it. There are many examples of people making large amounts of money from blogging. And why not? These people are also very skilled at generating buzz, otherwise their blogs wouldn't succeed. But beyond that, the media tends to portray this as the easiest and most common path to success for blogging. After reading the interviews in this book, you'll quickly realize that this isn't always the case. Monetizing a blog is just one way of benefiting from a blog. There are other great ways to get a lot of value from your blog.

In any case, let's start with the monetization of a blog, that is generating revenue directly from the blog. One of the more obvious examples includes Darren Rowse (http://www.ProBlogger.net). He's definitely been very successful at monetizing his blog. Darren of course does a lot more than just monetize his blog, but nonetheless he is a great example of how to succeed if this is your goal.

Just to intercede a quick moment, you'll find that Darren's blog is the most referenced blog throughout all the interviews. He unmistakably does more than just maximize his revenues, he offers a lot of great and powerful advice on how to blog successfully. Not just how to blog successfully with monetization as your goal, but how to blog successfully with any goal in mind. How to grow your traffic, how to increase the quality of your writing, etc. He's a great source of information, no one will go wrong reading and learning from his blog when they start out blogging themselves.

For others like myself, the goal is to personalize their companies. To talk about what happens within their company. To be transparent. To give a corporation a real face. To let people understand what happens behind the scenes, why it happens. It's a chance for them to share their beliefs, philosophies, war stories, etc. that they experience with their companies. And by doing so it attracts customers. A phenomenal example of this type of success is Joel Spolsky and his blog JoelOnSoftware.com. His blog is a seminal blog on software development. So many people refer to it, quote it, comment about it, basically devour it, that every time he has something to say, others will write about it. But more importantly, it has brought his company FogCreek to the limelight. His blog, or his articles (he created his site before blogging was really a term), helped sell his software.

Another common goal of blogging is to create expertise and authority for someone. You'll notice from many of the interviews in this book that many bloggers create their own expertise. They share their thoughts and knowledge, their experiences, everything they've learned. They become figureheads in their domains.

Seth Godin is a good example of someone who's been really successful at creating expertise in his domain through his blog. It of course helps that he's written numerous books, but as you'll find when you read the interviews, a lot of people recommend reading his blog. I'm also one of those people who religiously reads his blog. It's a great source of information. And because of this fact, the concept goes something like "if he writes about it he must also know a lot about it".

Patrick McKenzie states it eloquently in his blog post: "Why I Don't Monetize This Blog" (http://microisvjournal.wordpress.com/2008/02/11/why-i-dont-monetize-this-blog/).

"Happily, the blog is sort of a portfolio of all the things I can do that your average Mediocre Programmer can't. This leads to people throwing all sorts of opportunities my way, which I'm always humbled and happy to receive. I have gotten, at last count, eight job offers from readers (but for the day job and my own business, I would probably have accepted several of them). My collaborations with Google on the Conversion Optimizer case study and with Steph on his blogging book both flowed pretty much directly from the trust I had built up here. Neither of those pays money, either, but they enhance my status as an expert and will make it easier to convince the next decision maker that I am the right guy for the job/opportunity/investment/whatever. (The bosses at my day job were also extraordinarily pleased with the Google thing, believing that having an "in" with Google is in their best interests. They have given me explicit permission to continue my uISV adventure since it keeps increasing my value to them, and that in itself is worth every hour I have spent on this blog and then some.)"

Beyond that I believe a lot of people write blogs simply because they enjoy it. There's something to be said about having a blog that people want to follow and read. Dale Carnegie wrote in his book "How to Win Friends & Influence People" that one of the strongest motivators of people is *a feeling of importance*. Being a successful blogger will definitely help you fulfill this motivation. You might not become world famous, but in your niche you might become a superstar, and that's what matters most to people. Getting respect and admiration from the people they most want it from. For example if you're a die-hard computer programmer, there's nothing as motivating as getting positive feedback from another amazing programmer.

Which leads us to these questions. Where is blogging heading? What is in its future? I personally believe blogging is here to stay. And like today, only a few bloggers will ever achieve the real level of success they expect. There will always be many people who will start blogs, but very few will last more than a few months. Those who do, and learn as they go, will succeed. And this is why I decided to write this book, to gather up the best advice from some of the best bloggers in the world into one book. Their advice is phenomenal and timeless. And this is why I suggest you read this book several times as you proceed through your blogging career. If you're just starting to blog, this book will be information overload. After you've been blogging for a while, when your level of blogging experience increases, you'll get a different appreciation for the interviews. And as time goes on I believe you will continue to reference this book for advice and inspiration.

Chapter 1

Aaron Wall

SEOBook

http://www.seobook.com

Aaron Wall is a well known blogger who primarily focuses on search engines, internet marketing, and why ideas spread. He is also the author of the eBook entitled "SEO Book" which has sold innumerable copies and is referenced throughout the internet.

Although Aaron is successful now, it has not always been easy for him. Early in his youth he was nearly legally blind, at least until half-way through high school without knowing it. Even through this adversity he still had a strong disposition towards entrepreneurship, most notably buying and selling baseball cards.

After graduating high school, Aaron joined the military as a nuclear reactor operator on a special operation fast attack submarine. However this was not the lifestyle for him for several reasons and he soon left the military. Upon leaving the military Aaron went through some rougher times and almost went bankrupt. This is when he took a job as a middle level manager.

He continued to work as a middle-level manager for almost a year while simultaneously learning everything he could about the web. He finally quit to focus on his web initiatives when he had reduced his debt to $10,000 and was making at least some money on the internet, which at the time was about $100/month. It didn't take him long to go from there to making $10,000 a month. Within a year (the end of 2004) he had achieved success! Since then he has only been growing his success.

Steph: What makes a blog successful according to you? Is it traffic, reach, revenue, etc.?

Aaron: It depends on the goals of the site. I have some blogs that make no money and have a low readership but help people, and to me those are successful. Other blogs are just about personal expression while my business ones are more income oriented. It is easy to get stuck on traffic stats, but you still have to pay your way.

Steph: When did you decide you finally reached success with your blog?

Aaron: I started my blog in December of 2003, started selling my eBook on it in February of 2004, and was fairly successful by April of 2004. I got started on the web in January of 2003.

Steph: How long does it take to become a successful blogger?

Aaron: I had a little known blog on my other site for about 3 months prior to creating SEO Book, so I guess it took about 7 months total. Though you don't really become successful overnight or at any set point in time. I think of being successful as being self funding and having the confidence necessary to keep learning and keep trying new things.

Steph: Who do you think are the most successful bloggers on the internet today?

Aaron: I think Seth Godin (**http://sethgodin.typepad.com/**) and Matt Cutts (**http://www.mattcutts.com/blog/**) have great influence. I love reading GapingVoid.com (**http://www.gapingvoid.com/**). I am mostly focused on internet marketing at the moment though, so my view of the web is a bit limited.

Steph: Which five blogs do you regularly read?

Aaron: I read every post Frank Schilling writes on his Seven Mile blog (**http://www.sevenmile.com/**). I am a regular reader of SearchEngineLand.com (**http://searchengineland.com/**). And while it is not updated as frequently as those two, I love TropicalSEO.com (**http://tropicalseo.com/**) by Andy Hagans. CopyBlogger.com (**http://www.copyblogger.com/**) and Paul Kedrosky (**http://paul.kedrosky.com/**) are equally refreshing.

Steph: Which websites would you recommend for any new bloggers starting to blog?

Aaron: Brian Clark's Copyblogger (**http://www.copyblogger.com/**) is a must read if you want to understand how to write compelling conversion oriented copy. Daren Rowse's ProBlogger.com (**http://www.problogger.com/**) is a must read if you want to get into understanding the mechanics of blogging. I also think you should read at least a dozen blogs about a topic you are interested in to learn how and why ideas spread amongst bloggers. Use iGoogle or Google Reader to make it easy to subscribe to a wide array of blogs.

Steph: Which book(s) would you recommend for new bloggers (these can range from marketing books, blogging books, etc.)?

Aaron: The Cluetrain Manifesto teaches you why the web is different than monolithic marketplaces of the past. Steven Krug's Don't Make Me Think teaches you about how to create a usable website. If you make a site that is usable and market demand oriented people are going to use it. Seth Godin's Purple Cow teaches you how to be remarkable. Links are nothing but citations or remarks. If you know how to be remarkable then marketing is easy.

Steph: What is your most successful blog post ever?

Aaron: As far as spreading on the web, I would have to say that posting about getting sued for blog comments went far. I also launched an SEO tool called SEO for Firefox. Beyond those, I don't think I have had any signature posts that I could easily point out as examples of successful posts. I actually had one article that did well before I became a popular blogger, but I think many of my posts are pretty good and I was lucky enough to enter a growing market early with a unique voice.

Steph: What's your biggest tip on writing a successful blog post?

Aaron: If you are new to blogging and want an idea to spread make sure you get community feedback early on such that market leaders in your industry have a vested interest in talking about your blog post.

Steph: What's your best advice in regards to content and writing for bloggers?

Aaron: It is easy to think that if you had one hit post that would get lots of readers, but people are fickle and competition is fierce. Doing well with blogging is not about writing one key post, it is about performing day after day and helping a few people at a time. Eventually big success comes out of all the smaller successes. Sometimes it arrives via an accident or mistake.

Steph: How important do you think are the headlines of your blog articles?

Aaron: Headlines are critical. They set the tone for the piece and a strong one can even change the mood of the reader before they even get to the content. Some social media sites will vote up a story based on the headline, without even bothering to read the story.

Steph: Do you spend any money and time on marketing?

Aaron: I have spent over $100,000 and over 3 years marketing my blog.

Steph: What are your main methods of marketing your blog?

Aaron: I have an affiliate program, I buy AdWords and AdSense ads, and I pay for a lot of custom programs that I give away. In turn, people link at my site and tools and talk about my site, which leads to more sales.

Steph: Which marketing tactic has surprised you the most in terms of its effectiveness?

Aaron: Just performing day in and day out. Making oneself available via email, blog comments, etc. allows you to make connections and build brand loyalists one person at a time.

Steph: What are your quick and short five best tips for blogging?

Aaron:

Link out to other interesting pages. Linking out is a form of free marketing, plus it prevents you from wasting time trying to create the web again from scratch.

Read and write everyday.

Write a second personal blog for family, political, and off topic posts.

Consume information in a variety of formats, including books, DVDs, magazines, and blogs.

Mix up your format. Use pictures, headers, and sub headers.

Steph: What is the most common pitfall new bloggers generally fall into?

Aaron: Many bloggers get burned out because they try to be too rigid following someone else's advice, and thus take the fun out of blogging or feel everything has already been said before.

Steph: If you knew what you know now when you first started, what's the one biggest tip you'd give yourself today?

Aaron: Re-invest more aggressively sooner.

Steph: What repels you the most from a blog (animations, in your face advertising, etc.)?

Aaron: AdSense ads plastered above the content on a blog with a default WordPress design. It basically says I don't care for you.

Steph: Do you make any direct money from your blog through advertising, product placements, etc.?

Aaron: I sell a bunch of eBooks. As an indirect revenue stream I sell consulting services.

Steph: What is your best monetization method (Ads, affiliate marketing, etc.)?

Aaron: Selling my own product far exceeds the profit potential for selling ads in my market. In the search marketing community most people are quite ad blind in nature, and there are only a few scalable business models that are willing to spend heavily on advertising across blogs.

Steph: Do you find you get more from direct monetization of your blog or from opportunities that come because of the existence of your blog?

Aaron: Right now I would say direct monetization is ahead, but I have lots of opportunities I am still building on. I just don't like to count checks until they are cashed.

Steph: What's your most interesting story related to your blog and blogging experience?

Aaron: My wife met me through buying my eBook. If I did not start my blog so she could find me I will still be a hollow lonely man.

Steph: What's the one biggest opportunity that came to you because of your blog?

Aaron: Getting married to my wonderful wife. I don't deserve to be with someone so wonderful. I need to work hard to become the person she deserves.

Steph: Any other comments or thoughts you'd like to share?

Aaron: Thanks for the interview Steph.

Chapter 2

Abdylas Tynyshov

AdesBlog.com

http://www.adesblog.com/

Abdylas (also known as Ades) was born in 1978 in Kyrgyz Republic, popularly known as Kyrgyzstan internationally. It's a tiny republic in Central Asia with a population of approximately 5 million people .It's one of the former 15 countries that gained independence after the collapse of USSR in 1991.

This important incident brought along a lot of opportunities to Kyrgyz people from the outside world. Suddenly lots of countries were opening businesses, schools, and universities in Kyrgyzstan. One of these schools was his high school, which was opened by Turkish educational organization called SEBAT, in conjunction with Kyrgyz Government.

After graduating from Kyrgyz-Turkish High School in 1996, Abdylas applied to International Islamic University, in Malaysia (IIUM). He was accepted to the Department of Information & Communications Technology (ICT). He then graduated from IIUM in 2002, and went straight into the IT Industry. Initially, he worked as a Web-Designer, with his last position being a Creative Lead. But after working for about 3 years, he decided to concentrate on his own projects and pursue his education. By this time he was running a few online projects generating some income, so much that in November 2005, he was officially self-employed.

Today Abdylas is doing his MBA at Management Centre of IIUM, majoring in Strategic Management. He is also actively involved in several personal projects, including his blog and a few other websites which generate over 2 million unique visitors a year combined.

Steph: What makes a blog successful according to you? Is it traffic, reach, revenue, etc.?

Ades: Personally I think the person behind the blog makes the blog successful. His or her ideas, expertise in certain field, his or her thoughts and predictions make the blog stand out from the crowd.

However on internet, mostly traffic, monthly revenue and the number of RSS subscribers determine the success of the blog. Not always, but most of the time.

Steph: When did you decide you finally reached success with your blog?

Ades: Success is very subjective. Personally I believe that I have a long way to go. Some people might consider me successful already, however I think I still have a lot to learn. So for me, success is a lifelong journey.

Steph: How long does it take to become a successful blogger?

Ades: It takes several months to fully grasp how various tools and technologies related to blogging work. It takes another few months to perfect your writing skills. So basically, it could take up to a year to be a successful blogger.

Steph: Who do you think are the most successful bloggers on the internet today?

Ades: It would be Darren Rowse of ProBlogger.net (**http://www.problogger.net/**) and John Chow of JohnChow.com (**http://www.johnchow.com/**).

Steph: Which five blogs do you regularly read?

Ades:

ProBlogger (**http://www.problogger.net/**)

Entrepreneur's Journey (**http://www.entrepreneurs-journey.com/**)

ShoeMoney (**http://www.ShoeMoney.com/**)

Doshdosh (**http://www.doshdosh.com/**)

TechCrunch (**http://www.techcrunch.com/**)

Steph: Which websites would you recommend for any new bloggers starting to blog?

Ades: I think Problogger.net (**http://www.problogger.net/**) is a great place to start. Darren has covered most of the blogging related things already.

Steph: Which book(s) would you recommend for new bloggers (these can range from marketing books, blogging books, etc.)?

Ades: I personally think you don't need to buy a book to learn how to blog. There are plenty of websites and blogs that teach you how to start your own blog for free. However new bloggers can consider this book "The Rough Guide to Blogging 1" by Rough Guides

Steph: What is your most successful blog post ever?

Ades: I have written a post (guide) on blog posting frequency that consists of three parts. It's one of my favorite posts. You can read it at http://www.adesblog.com/2007/10/06/guide-on-blog-posting-frequency/

Steph: What's your biggest tip on writing a successful blog post?

Ades: The first and foremost, the post must be useful to the reader.

Steph: What's your best advice in regards to content and writing for bloggers?

Ades: Always incorporate your own thoughts and analysis when blogging about particular issue or topic. Because at the end, it's your personal opinion that counts. Your thoughts and ideas are your competitive advantage that differentiates you and sets you apart from other bloggers.

Steph: How important do you think are the headlines of your blog articles?

Ades: Extremely important. Because people like to scan the headlines, especially the new visitors. Your regular readers might read the whole post from beginning till the end, but new visitors will often scan the headlines first. Thus it's important to have catchy and descriptive headlines that will turn these new visitors into regular readers.

Steph: Do you spend any money and time on marketing?

Ades: Yes, sometimes.

Steph: What are your main methods of marketing your blog?

Ades: Sometimes I would buy a banner advertisement from other blogs for a month or two. I have also used StumbleUpon's advertising service. Other than that, I try to concentrate on producing quality content. After all, it's the quality of the posts that matter the most (at least for me).

Steph: Which marketing tactic has surprised you the most in terms of its effectiveness?

Ades: StumbleUpon. If you have great content, you will be surprised how well StumbleUpon can perform. StumbleUpon can have the multiplier effect that other advertising programs don't. You can read more on this effect on my post titled "Effective advertising strategy using StumbleUpon" available at http://www.adesblog.com/2007/07/02/effective-advertising-strategy-using-stumbleupon/.

Steph: What are your quick and short five best tips for blogging?

Ades:

Blog in a category that you have expertise

Register your own domain name

Use WordPress, it has many advantages over other platforms

Blog in your own style, do not imitate others

Have a professional design for your blog

Steph: What is the most common pitfall new bloggers generally fall into?

Ades:

Start blogging on free blogging platforms like blogspot.com

Being carbon copy of popular bloggers i.e. talking exactly on topics that these popular bloggers are currently talking

Monetizing the blog too much, filling the blog with all sorts of advertisements

Steph: If you knew what you know now when you first started, what's the one biggest tip you'd give yourself today?

Ades: Register problogger.com and problogger.net (wink).

Steph: What repels you the most from a blog (animations, in your face advertising, etc.)?

Ades:

Too many ads inside the content.

Too many posts a day, anything more than 5 would be too much for me.

Steph: Do you make any direct money from your blog through advertising, product placements, etc.?

Ades: Yes. Most of my income comes from advertising, and some from paid reviews.

Steph: What is your best monetization method (Ads, affiliate marketing, etc.)?

Ades: Text links ads. Text-Link-Ads.com and LinkWorth.com has been working really well on my blog. But it might not be the case in the few months to come, because of Google's tough stance on paid links.

Another method is of course direct advertisements. This includes text links, banner ads, and paid reviews for me.

From affiliate marketing programs, Shutterstock.com has been doing really good for me. It's a website where people can sell their digital photos. When you refer people to ShutterStock.com, you get paid for every sale that the referred person makes.

Steph: Do you find you get more from direct monetization of your blog or from opportunities that come because of the existence of your blog?

Ades: At this point in time, definitely from the direct monetization methods

Steph: Thank you Ades for the interview.

Chapter 3

Al Carlton

Coolest-Gadgets.com

http://www.coolest-gadgets.com/

Up until 2004, Al Carlton was a full-time coder/programmer, designing and writing financial systems. During that year (2004) Al decided he wanted to leave the rat race and experimented with various web ventures. Towards the end of 2005 he created the blog Coolest-Gadgets.com which after a year of hard work was generating enough income to replace his salary and enable him to leave the 9-5 rat race. Today Al spends most of his time travelling and building his growing portfolio of websites and blogs.

Steph: What makes a blog successful according to you? Is it traffic, reach, revenue, etc.?

Al: With blogging success means different things to different people, for me a successful blog means traffic and revenue, the two of which are closely related, the more traffic you get the more revenue you can earn.

Steph: When did you decide you finally reached success with your blog?

Al: I've had an element of success but still have far to go (I hope). The pinnacle so far would be when my blog income overtook my 9-5 income (Jan 2007) and I was able to leave the rat race

Steph: How long does it take to become a successful blogger?

Al: I've known some bloggers really make a name for themselves and a decent blog in 6 months others can take a lot longer. From a revenue perspective I'd allow 12-24 months before expecting a decent return.

Steph: Who do you think are the most successful bloggers on the internet today?

Al: I think a lot of the successful bloggers have other sites and business as well as their blog. Darren Rowse or ProBlogger.net (**http://www.problogger.net/**) is probably one of the most successful purely from a blogging perspective.

Steph: Which websites would you recommend for any new bloggers starting to blog?

Al: Problogger.net (**http://www.problogger.net/**) would be a good place to start, I also like DailyBlogTips.com (**http://www.DailyBlogTips.com**).

Steph: What is your most successful blog post ever?

Al: It would probably be the the about a GPS tracker (**http://www.coolest-gadgets.com/20060405/really-cool-portable-gps-tracker/**) it's been viewed something like 100,000 times and has generated well in excess of $2K, not bad for 15 minutes work!

Steph: What's your biggest tip on writing a successful blog post?

Al: Research and be interested in what you're writing about.

Steph: What's your best advice in regards to content and writing for bloggers?

Al: Be unique and let your personality show.

Steph: How important do you think are the headlines of your blog articles?

Al: Very. The headline is the first and often only thing people see, so it needs to grab their attention and make them want to read more.

Steph: Do you spend any money and time on marketing?

Al: Normally no but for this Christmas season I have been promoting some of my product based posts by paying other bloggers to write about my post (with a link of course) and so far the results have been very good, more from the traffic off the search engines rather than traffic from the other blogs.

Steph: What are your main methods of marketing your blog?

Al: Mainly I rely on quality unique content to bring the visitors

Steph: Which marketing tactic has surprised you the most in terms of its effectiveness?

Al: The Digg.com front page that brought about 20K visitors in a day. That was nice and free.

Steph: What are your quick and short five best tips for blogging?

Al:

Be unique

Persevere

Network with fellow bloggers
Write about something you have a passion for
Interact with your readers

Steph: What is the most common pitfall new bloggers generally fall into?

Al: They expect instant results and when quit too early

Steph: If you knew what you know now when you first started, what's the one biggest tip you'd give yourself today?

Al: Start sooner, if you have an idea for a post do it ASAP.

Steph: What repels you the most from a blog (animations, in your face advertising, etc.)?

Al: Popup ads, plagiarized content, really crappy English (must be really bad as mine isn't great)

Steph: Do you make any direct money from your blog through advertising, product placements, etc.?

Al: Yes

Steph: What is your best monetization method (Ads, affiliate marketing, etc.)?

Al: On my gadget blog (**http://www.coolest-gadgets.com/**) it does best from ads, closely followed by affiliate sales. The most lucrative ad program for that site is AdSense which is closing in on $20K per month.

Steph: Do you find you get more from direct monetization of your blog or from opportunities that come because of the existence of your blog?

Al: The business blog SelfMadeMinds.com (**http://selfmademinds.com/**) has brought us a fair amount of opportunities with other companies whilst the blog itself makes very little.

Steph: What's your most interesting story related to your blog and blogging experience?

Al: Probably going to Vegas to cover the Consumer Electronics show which just happened to coincide with Adult Video Expo, I remember trying to get served at the bar surrounded by porn stars. I gave up waiting to be served in the end.

Steph: What's the one biggest opportunity that came to you because of your blog?

Al: The opportunity to quit the 9-5 rat race

Steph: Thank you for your answers Al.

Chapter 4

Alex Papadimoulis

The Daily WTF

http://www.TheDailyWTF.com

Alex Papadimoulis lives in Berea, Ohio. He is a managing partner at Inedo, LLC. which brings custom software solutions to small and mid-sized businesses and helps other software development organizations utilize best practices in their products.

He is also the creator of TheDailyWTF.com. It all began when he initially posted an entry entitled "Your Daily Cup of WTF" on his old blog in 2004, complaining about the quality of development at his then current employer. Three days later a reader suggested that Alex should start a new website dedicated exclusively to "bad code" postings, and a few days later he indeed went ahead and registered TheDailyWTF.com where he began posting stories from readers.

Within a few months the traffic exploded and he had to switch from self-hosting in his basement to a dedicated server. TheDailyWTF.com now receives approximately 5 million page views and 1.5 million unique visitors per month.

Steph: What makes a blog successful according to you? Is it traffic, reach, revenue, etc.?

Alex: Readership. With marketing and SEO, it's not a huge challenge to drive one-time click-throughs and traffic, but I think what's really important is a real readership. Folks who visit every day or two and read what content you have to offer.

Steph: When did you decide you finally reached success with your blog?

Alex: When I realized that I could no longer use the Internet at home due to all the bandwidth WTF was using up, and had to move the site from my basement-hosted server to a "real" dedicated server at hosting facility.

Steph: How long does it take to become a successful blogger?

Alex: A lot depends on luck and timing of course, but I'd estimate two to three years. At least, that's what I've seen from colleagues who now host successful blogs.

Steph: Who do you think are the most successful bloggers on the internet today?

Alex: I guess I'd have to refer to what the "authorities" say on the matter, Technorati.com (**http://www.Technorati.com**), Alexa.com (**http://www.Alexa.com**), etc.

Steph: Which five blogs do you regularly read?

Alex: In no particular order:

Old New Thing (**http://blogs.msdn.com/oldnewthing/**)

You've Been Haacked (**http://haacked.com/**)

Coding Horror (**http://www.codinghorror.com/blog/**)

Consumerist (**http://consumerist.com/**)

Fark (**http://www.fark.com/**).

Steph: Which book(s) would you recommend for new bloggers (these can range from marketing books, blogging books, etc.)?

Alex: None specifically on blogging, but any book that teaches one how to write better would certainly help.

Steph: What is your most successful blog post ever?

Alex: It's hard to say, especially by how I measure success (steady readership). But the one that comes to mind is a series of posts, the Virtudyne Saga (**http://worsethanfailure.com/Articles/Best_of_2006_0x3a__The_Virtudyne_Saga.aspx**). It was a four-parter that told of the rise and fall of one of the industry's worst software disasters.

Steph: What's your biggest tip on writing a successful blog post? As well what's your best advice in regards to content and writing for bloggers?

Alex: Write well and write consistently.

While a typo here or an improperly used word there may not seem like a big deal, it really hurts the overall quality of the publication.

Readers aren't nitpicky, but mistakes certainly come through in the writing. It gives it an "unfinished" and "rough" feel, and a lot of readers aren't looking for mediocre content.

As for consistency, generally speaking, no one wants to read a publication that's about cats one day and politics the next. It's important to stay on topic and write on deadline. If you want to write daily, then write daily. If it's weekly, then make sure to write once a week. Too little or too much variation on the schedule hurts, too.

Steph: How important do you think are the headlines of your blog articles?

Alex: At first, they're critical. In a sea of posts from other blogs, there's just no other way to grab someone's attention. But a title alone won't keep readers; good content is key.

And on that same line, a deceptive title doesn't help anyone: sure, readers will click it, but no one's going to come back, and eventually, no one will trust the blog.

Steph: Do you spend any money and time on marketing?

Alex: I've been fortunate not to have to do any marketing.

Steph: What are your quick and short five best tips for blogging?

Alex:

Write well

Write consistently

Be accurate

Develop policies

Take it seriously

Steph: What is the most common pitfall new bloggers generally fall into?

Alex: The biggest mistake that I've seen new bloggers make is meta- and link-blogging. Meta-blogging is writing about blogging ("sorry I haven't updated in a while, I promise to soon...") and link blogging is merely passing along a single link to another blog without any additional insight or commentary on the matter.

Steph: If you knew what you know now when you first started, what's the one biggest tip you'd give yourself today?

Alex: I would have told myself, "Are you sure you want to get in to this? It's going to be a lot of work, and take up a lot of your day, and will be almost impossible to get away from."

Steph: What repels you the most from a blog (animations, in your face advertising, etc.)?

Alex: Intrusive advertising.

Steph: Do you make any direct money from your blog through advertising, product placements, etc.? And if so what is your best monetization method (Ads, affiliate marketing, etc.)?

Alex: Yes, and by far the best has been ads.

Steph: Do you find you get more from direct monetization of your blog or from opportunities that come because of the existence of your blog?

Alex: It's hard to place a value on the opportunities, especially in my line of work (consulting). While I think it has certainly helped with networking, no one has come up to me and said, "I read your blog, I'd like to pay you for your services." Well, unless you count writing services—I certainly have had the opportunity to write articles for other publications as a result of blogging, but the rate for writing articles is certainly less than advertisements (and a whole lot more work).

Steph: What's the one biggest opportunity that came to you because of your blog?

Alex: As a direct result of the blog—probably the opportunity to write in other publications. I've written in a few books and magazines, and am a regular columnist for Redmond Developer News.

Steph: Thank you for your answers and taking this interview Alex.

Chapter 5

Andy Brice

Successful Software

http://www.successfulsoftware.net/

Andy Brice is the founder of the software company Oryx Digital Ltd. He is also the creator of the software called PerfectTablePlan (sold by Oryx Digital Ltd.), a table seating planner for weddings, banquets and dinners. In addition to this Andy writes a blog about developing and marketing software called SuccessfulSoftware.net. He makes his living from the sales of his software product PerfectTablePlan through his company.

The blog SuccessfulSoftware.net was originally a sideline to his main software business however it has since generated significant interest and traffic from the community. On it you will find many useful and interesting articles, especially if you're a small independent software vendor (ISV).

Steph: What makes a blog successful according to you? Is it traffic, reach, revenue, etc.?

Andy: It depends on what your objectives are for your blog. But obviously readership is important. I don't think there is much point writing something if no-one else reads it.

Steph: When did you decide you finally reached success with your blog?

Andy: I don't think I have reached that point yet. Getting lucky once doesn't count.

Steph: How long does it take to become a successful blogger?

Andy: Ask me again in a few years.

Steph: Who do you think are the most successful bloggers on the internet today?

Andy: Amongst the thousands of people blogging about software, I would guess that Joel Spolsky (**http://www.joelonsoftware.com/**) and Jeff Atwood (**http://www.codinghorror.com/**) are the most successful, in terms of readership and influence. They have very different styles, but their blogs are always very insightful, well written and entertaining. Although you could argue that Joel On Software isn't strictly a blog, because it doesn't have comments.

Steph: Which five blogs do you regularly read?

Andy: I track about 30 different blogs in my RSS reader, nearly all related to software development and marketing. It's tough to single out a few. But three that stand out for me are:

Joel On Software (**http://www.JoelOnSoftware.com**)

Coding Horror (**http://www.CodingHorror.com**)

Eric Sink (**http://www.EricSink.com**)

Steph: Which websites would you recommend for any new bloggers starting to blog?

Andy: None really. Blogging is far too incestuous as it is. Just write about things that you care about that you think other people will care about.

Steph: Which book(s) would you recommend for new bloggers (these can range from marketing books, blogging books, etc.)?

Andy: I haven't read any books about blogging, so I can't comment.

Steph: What is your most successful blog post ever?

Andy: I wrote a minor investigative piece showing that many software download sites were giving out bogus awards to get back links (**http://successfulsoftware.net/2007/08/16/the-software-awards-scam/**). I think every software author who submits to download sites knew this was going on, but I proved it by getting a page full of awards for a program that didn't even run (it was a renamed text file). I hoped a few hundred people might read the article, but the response was quite overwhelming.

It made it to the front page of Digg.com, Reddit.com and Slashdot and even got a mention in the Guardian newspaper. According to my WordPress stats it has had 157,000 hits in the three months since I wrote it, with 53,000 hits on the peak day. I hope that the article will make some small contribution to ending this ugly practice.

Steph: What's your biggest tip on writing a successful blog post?

Andy:

Write well.

Don't listen to people like me who got lucky once.

Steph: How important do you think are the headlines of your blog articles?

Andy: I think the headline is important to draw people in. But they won't stay long if the rest of the article isn't well written.

Steph: Do you spend any money and time on marketing?

Andy: Not really.

Steph: What are your main methods of marketing your blog?

Andy: I include a link to my blog in my email signature. That's it.

Steph: What is the most common pitfall new bloggers generally fall into?

Andy: Too much commentary and not enough content. Try to write something interesting, rather than comment on something someone else wrote.

Steph: Do you make any direct money from your blog through advertising, product placements, etc.?

Andy: I don't run ads on my blog and I always try to make clear any interests I might have.

So far I have managed a free t-shirt from Eric Sink, $10 in e-junkie referral fees and 2 additional sales of my PerfectTablePlan software. I don't think I will be retiring from writing software any time soon.

Steph: What's the one biggest opportunity that came to you because of your blog?

Andy: Writing a blog takes a lot of time and effort. I think most people who write a blog hope for something in return for their efforts. One of my goals is to raise the profile of the consulting side of my business. But I currently don't have any time to spare from PerfectTablePlan, so it's a long-term goal. Also I like writing. It's nice to be able to sound off about things you care about.

Steph: Any other comments or thoughts you'd like to share?

Andy: Register your own domain. Don't rely on a blogging service to provide one for you. It is very cheap, convenient and easy to use a free service, such as WordPress.com. They are also very well set-up to handle the inevitable traffic spike if you get 'slashdotted'. But it does come with its own risks. WordPress can shut down your blog without a warning, without a reason and without any right of appeal. It happened to my blog not long ago. Apparently it was an honest mistake on their part and they restored full access. But if they hadn't, at least I would have been able to redirect somewhere else from SuccessfulSoftware.net.

Chapter 6

Anita Campbell

Small Business Trends

http://www.smallbiztrends.com/

Anita Campbell is the CEO of Small Business Trends, providing information and intelligence about the small business market and business trends affecting that market.

Her flagship website is the award-winning Small Business Trends (http://www.smallbiztrends.com), named a Forbes Best of the Web, a CODIE 2007 finalist, and noted and written about in the Wall Street Journal and MSNBC television.

Anita is a prolific writer with articles and columns published at Inc Technology, BNET.com, Work.com, Online Merchant Network, and a variety of other sites and print publications. She is the host of Small Business Trends Radio, broadcasted over the Internet.

Before starting her own business, Anita held a variety of senior executive positions, culminating in the role of CEO of an information technology subsidiary of Bell & Howell. Anita holds a B.A. from Duquesne University and a J.D. from the University of Akron Law School.

Steph: What makes a blog successful according to you? Is it traffic, reach, revenue, etc.?

Anita: Three factors, in this order:

Influence and community—in blogs you have the luxury to cover subjects that large mainstream publications can't really cover—and you can cover them in a more personal style. This tends to increase the influence of a blog over mainstream pubs, because people identify with the style and the people behind the blog, and become members of a community. Once you achieve a community it can have a powerful influence.

Revenue—a business blog should lead to revenue, although it can be indirect. A blog can help with lead generation and in that indirect way can drive revenue.

Reach to niche audience—reach is important, but with blogs it's reach to a niche audience. So it's not just pure numbers, but rather whether you're reaching particular niche audience in sufficient numbers. Plus you have to consider the size of the niche market and the type of market. A blog could be extremely influential at 10,000 visitors a week—if it's the right 10,000.

Steph: When did you decide you finally reached success with your blog?

Anita: Success is a never ending journey, so I'm not finished yet! However, when I started receiving far more emails than I could comfortably handle, I knew I was making an impact. Success is a reflection of the demand for one's time and involvement.

Steph: How long does it take to become a successful blogger?

Anita: Unless you're backed by a substantial financial stake and can hire researchers, writers and marketers, it really takes a good two years to get established today. Blogs are an example of the network economy and the "law of increasing returns." At first the gains seem small, but as the network effect increases, it increases exponentially. So once a blog starts growing, the growth rate seems to accelerate.

Steph: Who do you think are the most successful bloggers on the internet today?

Anita: That depends on the markets they serve and the types of blogs they have. As a category, I've found blogs by entrepreneurs and small businesses to be successful compared to the size of the business—because a blog acts like a megaphone for the business.

Steph: Which five blogs do you regularly read?

Anita:

SearchEngineGuide.com (**http://www.searchengineguide.com/**)

TechCrunch.com (**http://www.techcrunch.com/**)

InstaPundit.com (**http://www.instapundit.com/**)

SmallBizTechnology.com (**http://www.smallbiztechnology.com/**)

SmallBizLabs.com (**http://www.smallbizlabs.com/**)

Steph: Which websites would you recommend for any new bloggers starting to blog?

Anita:

Read and study some blogs in your industry or covering the same or related topics

Sign up for a good RSS feed aggregator, such as **Bloglines.com** and subscribe to 20 or 30 different feeds

Then find your own style and just get out there and start doing

Steph: Which book(s) would you recommend for new bloggers (these can range from marketing books, blogging books, etc.)?

Anita: Get some good, regularly updated eBooks:

For SEO, either get SEOBook (**http://www.seobook.com/**) or Search Marketing for Small Businesses (by SearchEngineGuide.com).

For blogging as a business endeavor (i.e., to directly generate revenue) try Yaro Starak's Blog Mastermind course (**http://www.blogmastermind.com/**).

Subscribe to MarketingSherpa.com (**http://www. MarketingSherpa.com**) for great marketing insights.

As far as other blogging-related topics, my feeling is that if you are dedicated and spend time each week reading other blogs, you will learn the craft. Some of the most helpful, most specific and up-to-date information about blogging can be found online at other blogs. Print books on the topic tend to be either too general or may quickly be outdated.

Steph: What is your most successful blog post ever?

Anita: I've written a couple of thousand posts, so it's hard to point to just one. I'd say the most successful either have given very specific advice that is hard to find, or they've covered situations where I've provided some personal experiences.

Steph: What's your biggest tip on writing a successful blog post?

Anita: Choose the right title and you're at lest halfway there. Include a keyword (for search purposes) in a title, too. Think of how someone might search in a search engine to answer a question or research a purchase or solve a problem—mirror that in your title. This is not only good for getting the post listed in the search engines, but it tracks what is likely to appeal to readers.

Steph: What's your best advice in regards to content and writing for bloggers?

Anita: Write about what you know, and write original content as much as possible. Don't waste too much time quoting other articles, unless you also have something to add. And don't try to be like everyone else or a copycat. March to a different drummer.

Steph: How important do you think are the headlines of your blog articles?

Anita: Crucial—see above. They can make or break an article. If you only have time to learn one blogging technique, I'd say focus on learning how to write great titles that speak to your audience and their pain points or desires.

Steph: Do you spend any money and time on marketing?

Anita: I spend lots of time on marketing—wish I could spend more time. You can't expect to just write and have visitors come to you—that's too passive.

I have spent small amounts of money on marketing, running small Google AdWords campaigns and other techniques off and on. But my expenditures have not been large. But the hours I've invested are huge over the past four years.

Steph: What are your main methods of marketing your blog?

Anita: Commenting on other blogs; guest posting in a select few other blogs; writing guest articles for business newsletters; occasional emailing of posts to other bloggers (not more than once a month); participating in blog carnivals; inviting guest posts on my blog; treating PR people with respect and giving them interviews for their clients or radio show appearances for their clients and thanking them afterwards; practicing good SEO copywriting techniques when writing blog posts; some social media optimization.

Steph: Which marketing tactic has surprised you the most in terms of its effectiveness?

Anita: Treating PR people with respect and interviewing their clients—wish I had time and resources to do conduct and write up interviews twice a day—I'd do it in a New York minute. What happens is that companies who get interviewed often will link to your post from their press section, blog, newsletter or sometimes even their home page—or all of the above. So the investment of time (sometimes it takes 2 to 4 hours to do an interview, review a product and write an article) can pay off. Of course, this tip only works if your blog is in effect a magazine—if your blog is there primarily to generate leads for your business then this technique does not translate well.

Steph: What are your quick and short five best tips for blogging?

Anita: If your goal is for your blog to be highly trafficked and an 800-lb gorilla in your niche, then you must post once or twice a day—Technorati.com stats show that the most popular and influential blogs average two posts a day.

Hone your own style. I read style tips from other bloggers laid down as if they are hard and fast rules. But in reality, they amount to style preferences. One blogger may like posts that are quick, 200- to 300-word posts that are highly-opinionated. Another blogger might like to write objective data-rich essays of 750 to 1000 words. There's no right or wrong—just make it fit your purpose and your audience. Example: if you're writing a celebrity blog, readers probably do not want long essays filled with statistics. On the other hand, if you're writing an economics blog, you'll have more credibility with that audience if you write essays with detailed charts.

Chunk your content for the Web: Keep the chunks small visually, so that the eye can take them in. (Note: this is not the same as style—this is for readability on the Web where there is not as much contrast as the printed page.) Sentences between 10 and 25 words. Paragraphs between 3 and 5 sentences max. Liberal use of bullet points. Use of an image to break up large expanses of text and grab the eye's attention.

SEO your posts. This means you must use a keyword in your posts. Generally you should use a keyword in the title; 2 or 3 times minimum in the post body; in tags in your post; and in alt tags for the accompanying image.

Try to post early in the day, by 7:00 am EST if you can. This ensures that the widest English-speaking audience across time zones will view your content as "fresh." It can make as much as 10% difference in traffic.

Steph: What is the most common pitfall new bloggers generally fall into?

Anita: Wanting instant gratification and getting discouraged after 30 days. Building an audience and standing out from the crowd take time and hard work.

Steph: If you knew what you know now when you first started, what's the one biggest tip you'd give yourself today?

Anita: Don't stay on a free or hosted service longer than 90 days. For instance, don't stay on Blogger, Wordpress.com, or TypePad for long. If you really plan on blogging in a serious way, you need to host the blog with your own arrangements at your own domain URL. If you wait too long you end up starting all over again when you finally move—moving disrupts everything: your existing inbound links; PageRank; Technorati rank, RSS subscribers; and similar metrics.

Steph: What repels you the most from a blog (animations, in your face advertising, etc.)?

Anita: Finding something I didn't expect to find on a blog, such as a business blog that makes political statements. If I want business, I'll go to a business blog. If I want politics, I'll go to a political blog. But don't mix the two.

Steph: Do you make any direct money from your blog through advertising, product placements, etc.?

Anita: Yes.

Steph: What is your best monetization method (Ads, affiliate marketing, etc.)?

Anita: In this order:

Flat fee sponsorships (i.e. $xx per month for sponsorship rights)

Banner ads

Text link ads (with no follow tags, of course)

Selected affiliate programs

Google AdSense—I've never made much from AdSense, and consider them filler ads when I don't have other ads filling the ad slots.

Steph: Do you find you get more from direct monetization of your blog or from opportunities that come because of the existence of your blog?

Anita: Opportunities that come from existence of the blog. But interestingly, that was not my goal. I was hoping that the blog would get me out of selling "time" and help me avoid doing consulting. I wanted to make money while I slept. But I find that the more popular the blog becomes, the more companies want to hire my services for consulting and speaking. I don't even prospect for services work—it comes to me. But all due to the visibility and reputation established on the blog.

Steph: What's your most interesting story related to your blog and blogging experience?

Anita: I put up a SitePal avatar which looks like me because it was designed from my photograph. A former colleague from my corporate days ten years ago was so taken by the avatar that he emailed me. Turns out, he had been a regular reader of my blog but I hadn't known it. It took the avatar to break the ice and get him to touch base with me. Now his company is a client of mine.

Steph: What's the one biggest opportunity that came to you because of your blog?

Anita: The opportunity to work with companies like American Express OPEN and Intuit. As a small business owner, I can't imagine figuring out how to break into companies like those, were it not for my visibility established from the blog.

Steph: Thank you Anita for taking this interview.

Chapter 7

Asha Dornfest

Parent Hacks

http://www.ParentHacks.com/

Asha Dornfest is the founder and publisher of Parent Hacks, a site devoted to parents' scrappy, real-world tips and product recommendations.

Starting a blog was a natural outgrowth of Asha's background in writing and technology. Before the Web was in popular use and well before kids, she and her husband Rael started a "Web design" business. In the early 90s, if you knew HTML, you were practically a Web designer by default. From there, Asha went on to write several computer how-to manuals, including "For Dummies" titles about Web publishing.

After her kids were born, her interest and writing inspiration turned to parenting, not because she felt a sense of expertise—in fact, just the opposite. Parenting was the first endeavor Asha undertook in which "reading the manual" had no effect, and, in some cases, made things harder. She started Parent Hacks as a place where parents could find those priceless tidbits of "worked for me" parenting advice one usually stumbled upon by chance—stuff that rarely showed up in the "expert" parenting manuals lining her bookshelves. Along the way, she discovered a generous and smart community of parents all of whom understand that when enough of us throw a bit of wisdom into the pot, it gets easier for all of us.

Asha is the mother of two children (an eight-year-old son and a four-year-old daughter), and the wife of a "charming and brilliant geek". They live in Portland, Oregon.

Steph: What makes a blog successful according to you? Is it traffic, reach, revenue, etc.?

Asha: Traffic, reach, and revenue are all metrics that can be measured so they get a disproportionate amount of attention. They're important numbers. Absolutely. But even though I'm working on ways to make those numbers grow, I don't actually think they are the most important indicators of success. Nothing like leading with a cliché, but I'll do it anyway: a successful blog (or publication or business) improves the lives of its readers. That may mean supplying a time-saving tip, saving readers money, or making them laugh. Whatever...if a blog improves the lives of its readers, they'll keep coming back, and when they do, the traffic, reach and revenue will follow.

Steph: When did you decide you finally reached success with your blog?

Asha: Reached success? Hmmm, I don't think success is an end point, really. That said, I'm thrilled with my readers' level of enthusiasm and involvement. I've always enjoyed the role of community facilitator, and I feel like that's what I've become at Parent Hacks. It's more than a one-way blog...it's a conversation.

Steph: How long does it take to become a successful blogger?

Asha: There's no way to quantify the time it takes, although folks in it for the long haul certainly have an advantage. Parent Hacks is one of those unusual cases of a site taking off almost as soon as it launched (disgusting, I know.). I wish I could take all the credit and say that it was my brilliant forethought and subtle design, but serendipity played a big part.

Steph: Who do you think are the most successful bloggers on the internet today?

Asha: My role models are Leo Babauta (**http://zenhabits.net/**), J. D. Roth (Getting Rich Slowly: **http://getrichslowly.org/blog/**) and Merlin Mann (43 Folders: **http://www.43folders.com/blog**). Each writes a highly-engaging blog with a distinctive voice. Each built authoritative blogs because they wanted to improve an aspect of their own lives, and then share what they learned with the world. That generosity comes across in every page. None of these writers rests on the laurels of a "successful site;" they're always looking for ways to give readers useful, well-written content. While each of these writers earns revenue from their sites, and is open about it, money never feels like the purpose of the blog. The bottom line is almost too simple: I like each of these people a lot.

Steph: Which five blogs do you regularly read?

Asha:

Confessions of a Pioneer Woman [hilarious and oddly exotic]
(**http://www.thepioneerwoman.com/**)

Cool Mom Picks [stylish and smart] (**http://www.coolmompicks.com/**)

Ask Moxie [useful and generous] (**http://moxie.blogs.com/askmoxie/**)

TechCrunch [I can't help myself] (**http://www.techcrunch.com/**)

Sweet Juniper! [most likely to bring a tear to my eye] (**http://www.sweet-juniper.com/**)

Steph: Which websites would you recommend for any new bloggers starting to blog?

Asha:

Problogger [of course] (**http://www.problogger.net/**)

Creating Passionate Users [there's gold in them thar archives] (**http://headrush.typepad.com/**)

Micro Persuasion [super-intelligent commentary on social communication] (**http://www.micropersuasion.com/**)

Seth's Blog [because everyone should read Seth Godin] (**http://sethgodin.typepad.com/**)

Steph: Which book(s) would you recommend for new bloggers (these can range from marketing books, blogging books, etc.)?

Asha: I find that books on blogging generally lag too far behind the info available online. On the other hand, marketing books, with Seth Godin's books standing out in particular, are good reminders that our blogs are, indeed, worthy of great content AND good promotion.

Steph: What is your most successful blog post ever?

Asha: Hard to judge, really. The post I'm most proud of is the one in which I shared the story of an American grandmother stationed in Iraq who collected toys and distributed them to children she met there (**http://www.parenthacks.com/2006/09/spread_the_word.html**). I encouraged Parent Hacks readers, along with all the bloggers I knew, to spread the word and donate toys, and we managed to create an incredible toy drive. People were so happy to be able to do something positive in the face of a terrible situation.

Steph: What's your biggest tip on writing a successful blog post?

Asha: Economical writing. Follow those journalism rules—lead with a strong hook, and only write as much as you need to. But don't make it so sparse that it feels impersonal. Readers should never wonder if there's a person behind the blog. Bonus tip: if you're funny, use humor. If you're not (be honest), stick to useful.

Steph: What's your best advice in regards to content and writing for bloggers?

Asha: Good writing counts. Connect with your readers.

Steph: How important do you think are the headlines of your blog articles?

Asha: Exceedingly important, both for time-challenged RSS subscribers and for a good showing in search engines.

Steph: Do you spend any money and time on marketing?

Asha: No money (except a few hundred bucks on business cards and a great logo), but I should spend more time. I've really focused on community-building rather than on expanding the audience.

Steph: What are your main methods of marketing your blog?

Asha: These would be my main methods if I spent the time I should on marketing: reaching out to print pubs, swapping posts with other sites, and just reaching out to people whose work I admire—that's something I do naturally because I'm so interested in how people do things. I toy with working the Diggs and Facebooks of the world, but I never stick with it.

Steph: Which marketing tactic has surprised you the most in terms of its effectiveness?

Asha: One thing I'm terrible at is analyzing my stats and testing my site improvements. As soon as people start asking me these sorts of questions I start stuttering. The quality that has likely made Parent Hacks as successful as it is—my focus on content and community—may bite me down the road, because I don't do anything with the pile of Google Analytics data I've got right in front of me.

Steph: What are your quick and short five best tips for blogging?

Asha:

Read Strunk and White's "Elements of Style."

Open your eyes to the world...soon you'll be following every observation with "I've got to blog about this."

Email your readers. If you don't have any, email writers you admire (briefly, they're busy). Jump in!

Don't neglect your life offline.

Get your own domain name.

Steph: What is the most common pitfall new bloggers generally fall into?

Asha: Trying to affect a cynical, snarky blog persona. I can't STAND authors who throw around the negativity in an effort to appear intelligent or edgy. Come to think of it, I don't like people who do that in real life, either.

Steph: If you knew what you know now when you first started, what's the one biggest tip you'd give yourself today?

Asha: Get help.

Steph: What repels you the most from a blog (animations, in your face advertising, etc.)?

Asha: Bad writing.

Steph: Do you make any direct money from your blog through advertising, product placements, etc.?

Asha: Yep. Advertising (through Federated Media, Google AdSense and Feedburner) and Amazon Associates affiliate fees.

Steph: What is your best monetization method (Ads, affiliate marketing, etc.)?

Asha: Depends on the time of year, but my Amazon earnings have had the biggest growth curve.

Steph: Do you find you get more from direct monetization of your blog or from opportunities that come because of the existence of your blog?

Asha: I've gotten lots of offers (paid blogging jobs, book projects, etc.) as a result of my blogging, but I've turned almost all of them down in order to focus on my site.

Steph: What's your most interesting story related to your blog and blogging experience?

Asha: Once again, the Iraq toy drive that happened as a result of a Parent Hacks post. It is so humbling to think that there are little children in Iraq, many of whom are orphans, that have toys, clothes and supplies as a result of my spending a couple of hours writing a post and emailing people from the comfort of my dining room. I don't relate this story to pump up my self-importance, but to point out the amazing connective power blogs can have.

Steph: What's the one biggest opportunity that came to you because of your blog?

Asha: The chance to collaborate on a book with one of the most well-respected pediatricians in the country.

Steph: Any other comments or thoughts you'd like to share?

Asha: I just want to thank you for including me in this fascinating project! I can't wait to hear what your other interviewees have to say. I still have so much to learn.

Oh—one last rah-rah. I just want to encourage folks who want to write anything to start blogging. For us extroverted writers, the isolation that comes with writing is often the most difficult part. While blogging still happens behind a computer, it thrusts you into a fascinating community of people, many of whom may even become friends.

Chapter 8

Ben Casnocha

My Startup Life

http://mystartuplife.com/

Ben is one of the younger bloggers in this book, being only 20 years of age. However don't think his age has anything do to with lack of world experience. By the age of 14 he had already founded his second company, Comcate.

Unlike most other high school students who skip school to have fun, Ben was sneaking away from school for early morning flights to visit prospective clients. This is all the while captaining his high school basketball team and editing the school newspaper!

Ben has been featured on CNN Headline News, TechTV, and profiled in SF Weekly. He has spoken at Stanford University and many other business forums.

Above this, Ben has also written the book "My Start-up Life" which is full of specific and actionable advice for any and all entrepreneurs.

Steph: What makes a blog successful according to you? Is it traffic, reach, revenue, etc.?

Ben: For me, it's influence. I want my ideas to spread.

Steph: When did you decide you finally reached success with your blog?

Ben: When people told me I changed their opinion on something. That's influence.

Steph: How long does it take to become a successful blogger?

Ben: Depends. It takes several months to get in the groove and attract an audience.

Steph: Who do you think are the most successful bloggers on the internet today?

Ben: I look up to Jeff Jarvis (**http://www.buzzmachine.com/**), Brad Feld (**http://www.feld.com/blog/**), Tyler Cowen (**http://www.marginalrevolution.com/**), and others.

Steph: Which five blogs do you regularly read?

Ben:

Marginal Revolution (**http://www.MarginalRevolution.com/**)

Feld Thoughts (**http://www.feld.com/blog/**)

Overcoming Bias (**http://www.OvercomingBias.com/**)

BuzzMachine (**http://www.BuzzMachine.com/**)

Infectious Greed (**http://paul.kedrosky.com/**)

Steph: What is your most successful blog post ever?

Ben: I wrote a popular post on "What Society Overcomplicates" (**http://ben.casnocha.com/2007/02/what_does_socie.html**). I argued that parenting and writing are two examples of things which are really really hard—but simple. And that society tends to overcomplicate both these tasks.

Steph: What's your biggest tip on writing a successful blog post?

Ben: Be brief, be interesting, be personal.

Steph: How important do you think are the headlines of your blog articles?

Ben: Imported but overrated. Actual content is more important.

Steph: Do you spend any money and time on marketing?

Ben: Not really.

Steph: What are your main methods of marketing your blog?

Ben: Word of mouth, commenting on other blogs.

Steph: Which marketing tactic has surprised you the most in terms of its effectiveness?

Ben: How powerful a link from a popular blog can be.

Steph: What are your quick and short five best tips for blogging?

Ben:

Be it on for the long term

Write for yourself as much as for others

Be personal

Write well

Have fun

Steph: What is the most common pitfall new bloggers generally fall into?

Ben: Give up after a couple weeks since they feel no one is reading it. It takes time!

Steph: What repels you the most from a blog (animations, in your face advertising, etc.)?

Ben: Posts which say, "I haven't posted in 10 minutes and received 20 emails about whether I was still alive. Yes, I'm still alive, just really busy!" If you're too busy to post, then don't post. Just don't talk about how busy you are.

Steph: Do you make any direct money from your blog through advertising, product placements, etc.?

Ben: Some off advertising.

Steph: Do you find you get more from direct monetization of your blog or from opportunities that come because of the existence of your blog?

Ben: Definitely related opportunities. By a HUGE factor. Most of the monetization is indirect.

Steph: What's your most interesting story related to your blog and blogging experience?

Ben: I traveled through 20 countries overseas and in many big cities stayed with readers of my blog. Stayed in their house, that is. A wonderful experience.

Steph: What's the one biggest opportunity that came to you because of your blog?

Ben: The platform I have because of my blog probably helped convince a publisher to offer me a contract to write my book My Start-Up Life.

Steph: Thank you Ben for your time in taking this interview.

Chapter 9

Benjamin Yoskovitz

Instigator Blog

http://www.InstigatorBlog.com

Benjamin Yoskovitz is a 10-year veteran of startups and entrepreneurship. He started his first company in 1996 while studying Psychology at McGill University. His focus has always been on technology and Web-related companies. His expertise is in building successful businesses from the ground up, as well as helping others to do the same.

Benjamin started his blog, Instigator Blog in 2006 and continues to blog regularly about startups, entrepreneurship, business, marketing and technology.

He is now also CEO & co-founder of a startup in the recruiting space called Standout Jobs.

Steph: What makes a blog successful according to you? Is it traffic, reach, revenue, etc.?

Benjamin: It depends on what goals you set out for your blog in the first place. The most common goal is to make money. A lot of people see blogging as a "get rich quick" scheme, and that's certainly not the case. But, lots of people are making money from blogging, although very few, comparatively, are earning a living.

My preference, in terms of defining success, is based on the reach and influence you can have through your blog, as well as the opportunities your blog brings you as an authority (in whatever space you're in.)

Steph: When did you decide you finally reached success with your blog?

Benjamin: My blog feels like a success each and every time it brings me a new opportunity that I otherwise would not have gotten. That might be as "small" an opportunity as meeting someone new (that otherwise would have been much more difficult to reach), or as "big" as generating significant consulting and speaking opportunities.

Steph: How long does it take to become a successful blogger?

Benjamin: It takes forever. Blogging successfully—like being successful in business—is not an end goal, it's a process.

Steph: Who do you think are the most successful bloggers on the internet today?

Benjamin: There are too many to name. Certainly, there are a number of bloggers that make big money, and as much as making money from blogging fascinates me, it's not my own goal (at least with Instigator Blog.)

So, I'd say:

Darren Rowse from ProBlogger (**http://www.ProBlogger.com**)—He remains a leader in the "blogging about blogging" world. Lots of people have followed, but no one comes close to his success.

Brian Clark from CopyBlogger (**http://www.CopyBlogger.com**)—He's been my writing guru. One of my "secrets" to success has been following his series of posts on writing great headlines. That's not exactly a secret, of course, but surprisingly few people really follow what he writes.

Liz Strauss from Successful Blog (**http://www.successful-blog.com**)—She's a force to be reckoned with when it comes to building relationships through blogging. Heck, there's an entire conference (SOBCon) named after and dedicated to her.

Fred Wilson from AVC (**http://avc.blogs.com/**)—He's setting the mark for venture capitalists that blog, and as an entrepreneur with a startup, this is great for me. And I bet Fred would tell you that his blogging has led to many interesting opportunities.

Maki from Dosh Dosh (**http://www.doshdosh.com/**)—He's had one of the most meteoric rises as a blogger in the social media/blogging/online marketing worlds. Every post is detailed and thought provoking. I wish I could write like that.

Steph: Which five blogs do you regularly read?

Benjamin: I read over 100 blogs regularly, but here are 5 choices:

TechCrunch (**http://www.TechCrunch.com/**)—It's still one of the top resources for news on Web 2.0 startups and Internet technology companies. I also track:

VentureBeat (http://www.VentureBeat.com/) , Mashable (http://mashable.com/) , BlogNation (http://www.BlogNation.com/) and CenterNetworks (http://www.CenterNetworks.com/) which are all in the same vein.

JobMatchBox (http://www.JobMatchBox.com/)—This is an incredible blog on the recruiting and HR space, which is of particular interest to me because of my startup, Standout Jobs.

eMomsAtHome (http://www.eMomsAtHome.com/blog)—Wendy is an amazing person and blogger. And don't let the title of her blog dissuade you; she's a master of Internet marketing, blogging, social media and much, much more. Wendy provides me insight and inspiration. Plus, she's a friend.

Daily Blog Tips (http://www.DailyBlogTips.com/)—A great blog about blogging by Daniel Scocco.

Cheezhead (http://www.Cheezhead.com)—Another killer blog about recruiting, and specifically the online recruiting world.

Steph: Which websites would you recommend for any new bloggers starting to blog?

Benjamin: I've already mentioned some, but here's a list:

Copyblogger (http://www.copyblogger.com)

ProBlogger (http://www.problogger.net)

Daily Blog Tips (http://www.dailyblogtips.com)

Dosh Dosh (http://www.doshdosh.com)

Chris Brogan (http://www.chrisbrogan.com)

Andy Beard (http://www.andybeard.eu)

eMomsAtHome (http://www.emomsathome.com/blog)

Successful-Blog (http://www.successful-blog.com)

Lorelle on WordPress (http://lorelle.wordpress.com)—not just about WordPress, great for beginner bloggers

Steph: What is your most successful blog post ever?

Benjamin: Depends on how you define success. If you're basing it on traffic, there are a few that stand out:

9 Signs the Online Job Market is Broken (http://www.instigatorblog.com/9-signs-the-online-job-market-is-broken/2007/02/26/)

10 Essential Business Leadership Skills (http://www.instigatorblog.com/10-essential-business-leadership-skills/2007/04/16/)

Top 10 Reasons Why Proposals Fail (**http://www.instigatorblog.com/top-10-reasons-why-proposals-fail/2007/02/07/**)

One of my favorites is—How-To Start a Company and Family at the Same Time (**http://www.instigatorblog.com/how-to-start-a-company-and-family-at-the-same-time/2007/07/11/**). For starters, it's quite personal, and it also uses a different format than most blog posts, relying heavily on images.

Steph: What's your biggest tip on writing a successful blog post?

Benjamin: Write a great headline.

Steph: What's your best advice in regards to content and writing for bloggers?

Benjamin: This is basic advice on how to write a good blog post. But even though it's basic, people still don't follow it well. I try and follow these tips religiously (even if I don't succeed all the time!)

Stick to your niche (you've picked a niche, right?)

Write a great headline

Format posts well—use images, use sub-headlines, use bold & italics and other font treatments

Edit content vigorously before publishing it

Link to other bloggers often

Steph: Do you spend any money and time on marketing?

Benjamin: I don't spend any money, but I do spend lots of time marketing. Of course, we need to define marketing:

Building relationships with other bloggers (start by linking to others and commenting on other blogs)

Using social media and social bookmarking sites (i.e. Digg, StumbleUpon, etc.)

Writing guest posts on other blogs (which I've done on Pronet Advertising and Copyblogger)

I don't have any issues with spending money on marketing, but generally I think it's hard to buy an audience.

I do think you should spend money on your blog design if you can't design a great blog on your own.

Steph: Which marketing tactic has surprised you the most in terms of its effectiveness?

Benjamin: I'm still surprised, from time to time, by the eagerness and willingness of the blogging community to help other people (including me.) The concept of "reciprocity" is still strong within the blogosphere.

Steph: What are your quick and short five best tips for blogging?

Benjamin:

Write great content (Ha! That's a huge tip...)

Interact with others—You can't blog by yourself and expect people to find you

Link to others frequently

Learn about social media/social bookmarking and how to take advantage of those

Build one on one relationships with authorities in the blogging world (and in your niche) before you focus on building lots and lots of traffic.

Make sure you have a good blog design (Yes; design matters.)

Register a domain name

Steph: What is the most common pitfall new bloggers generally fall into?

Benjamin: There are a few:

Obsessing over traffic. It's hard to not study your traffic numbers on a minute-by-minute basis, but try not to get overwhelmed by the lack of traffic your blog might get initially.

Thinking that blogging is easy. It's not. It takes lots of effort, planning, networking, etc.

Not linking to other blogs in an effort to keep visitors from leaving.

Writing poor headlines.

Focusing on monetization too quickly.

Steph: If you knew what you know now when you first started, what's the one biggest tip you'd give yourself today?

Benjamin: There are two:

Know what you want to talk about. I started blogging without knowing what niche I'd focus on. In fact, I still don't focus on a specific niche, but I've learned to live with that. It's just the way my blog works; but I know it could be more successful from a traffic perspective if it was more focused. I write about multiple niches because I have multiple interests and my blog is designed to increase my own reach and improve my personal brand in those subjects.

Write better headlines.

Steph: What repels you the most from a blog (animations, in your face advertising, etc.)?

Benjamin:

Too much advertising.

A crappy design

Lousy writing (including dull headlines)

Steph: Do you make any direct money from your blog through advertising, product placements, etc.?

Benjamin: Yes, but very little. I don't focus on monetization since it's not the point of the blog.

Steph: Do you find you get more from direct monetization of your blog or from opportunities that come because of the existence of your blog?

Benjamin: I make more money from opportunities that come because of the existence of the blog, without a doubt. That's because my blog is designed to bring me opportunities beyond blog monetization.

Steph: What's the one biggest opportunity that came to you because of your blog?

Benjamin: My startup, Standout Jobs, can be traced back to blogging. I started my blog in an effort to build some name recognition and personal brand in the spheres of entrepreneurship and business. As a result of blogging, I went out to some local blogger meetings and other tech meetups in Montreal. I met my co-Founders in Standout Jobs at those meetings. So, by virtue of starting a blog, I ended up with more opportunities to network locally, and was able to meet the people I started Standout Jobs with. If that doesn't show you the power of blogging, nothing will.

Steph: Any other comments or thoughts you'd like to share?

Benjamin: Blogging isn't for everyone. But it's one of the most effective ways for people and businesses of building authority, name recognition and personal brand. It's one of the most effective ways at building up opportunities for yourself—locally and from all over the world.

Steph: Thank you for taking the interview Benjamin.

Chapter 10

Bob Walsh

47 Hats

http://www.47Hats.com

Bob Walsh is a cross between blogger and author (Clear Blogging and Micro-ISV:From Vision to Reality), a consultant helping microISVs and startups succeed through 1-to-1 consulting on product/company blogging, and a product positioning and microISV entrepreneur.

As a microISV'er, Bob is the founder of MasterList Professional, a Windows personal task and project manager. As well Bob is involved with Project X which is currently in stealth mode (some details are available through his blog).

In addition to 47Hats, Bob is also the author of the blogs ClearBlogging (http://www.clearblogging.com/) and To Do Or Else (http://www.todoorelse.com/).

Steph: What makes a blog successful according to you? Is it traffic, reach, revenue, etc.?

Bob: Depends on what you want from your blog. If you're a microISV—or a regular company for that matter—you want your blog to be a conversation with your current and prospective customers, a source of valuable information to them about that part of the world your product lives in. It's not about ad revenue—there shouldn't be anything like an ad on your blog.

If you're talking about blogging professionally, it's all about traffic because traffic drives ad revenue and that's what keeps food on the table. But you have to really, really care about what you're focusing on in your blog—every week there's a thousand "I'm going to be rich by blogging" blogs started; 990 are dead within a month.

The key to traffic is providing value to your readers. Whether that's through finding value out there and bringing it back to your readers, sharing your experience/insight/questions, or whatever approach you take.

Steph: When did you decide you finally reached success with your blog?

Bob: 2009. Seriously, my blogs are a work in progress, and I have miles to go with each before I'd say I've really done what I've set out to do.

Steph: How long does it take to become a successful blogger?

Bob: Minimum of 3 months, more like 9—Tim Ferriss (**http://www.fourhourworkweek.com**) is the exception that proves the rule.

Steph: Who do you think are the most successful bloggers on the internet today?

Bob: In the parts of the blogosphere I focus on (productivity, tech, marketing and digital life) Tim Ferriss (**http://www.fourhourworkweek.com**), Guy Kawasaki (**http://blog.guykawasaki.com/**), and Seth Godin (**http://sethgodin.typepad.com**) and Leo Babauta (**http://zenhabits.net**) have all catapulted to the top of the blog food chain, done so quickly, and sustain their leads through the force of their passion and creatively.

Steph: Which five blogs do you regularly read?

Bob: About 400, actually. But the blogs that are on my must read list right now, the blogs I make time to read not just scan are:

Escape from Cubicle Nation (**http://www.EscapeFromCubicleNation.com**)

Scoble's shared feed (**http://www.Scobleizer.com**)

Seth Godin (**http://sethgodin.typepad.com**)

Think Simple. Be Decisive (**http://thinksimplenow.com**)

Skelliewag (**http://www.skelliewag.org**)

Steph: Which websites would you recommend for any new bloggers starting to blog?

Bob: One blog rules: Darren Rowse's Problogger.net (**http://www.Problogger.net**). This is THE blog to read: be prepared to spend a week or so reading and absorbing Darren's great information.

Steph: Which book(s) would you recommend for new bloggers (these can range from marketing books, blogging books, etc.)?

Bob: Well, since you asked...Clear Blogging, by yours truly. What I set out to do in Clear Blogging is give someone who is brand new to blogging an understanding of how the major moving parts of blogging work, why they should blog, the kinds of blogs that currently exist, and just how much impact they could have as a blogger. Judging by the emails I get, and reviews, I succeeded.

Steph: What's your biggest tip on writing a successful blog post?

Bob: In a nutshell, you've got to care about what you're writing. Passion is what makes a blog worth reading. I'm not talking about passion as in shouting, screaming; I'm talking about passion for a subject that makes you hot and eager to write.

Steph: What's your best advice in regards to content and writing for bloggers?

Bob: First, edit what you write. Go back, make sure the spelling and grammar work, and most of all make sure your ideas aren't getting tied up in a knot by your words. Second, find and refine techniques that work for you to keep a steady flow of words from your keyboard to your blog.

Steph: How important do you think are the headlines of your blog articles?

Bob: Not very. I know the SEO-centric people will tell you different, but I'm trying to telegraph to my readers in one line why (hopefully) the words I've written are worth their time, not to please Google.

Steph: Do you spend any money and time on marketing?

Bob: My blogs are my main marketing tools: the more I blog well, the more the phone rings and sales happen.

Steph: What are your main methods of marketing your blog?

Bob: Commenting—with value and passion—elsewhere and creating posts that the people I want to reach find valuable. Google does the rest.

Steph: Which marketing tactic has surprised you the most in terms of its effectiveness?

Bob: Guest posts—I've done guest posts for several blogs, most recently Lifehack.org (**http://www.lifehack.org/**). Each guest post lead to a jump in readership.

Steph: What are your quick and short five best tips for blogging?

Bob:

Be passionate.

Be polite—trashing others comes back to haunt you.

Be pragmatic—don't try to create perfect posts, you won't succeed.

Be persistent—count on 4 months of obscurity before you get traction.

Be proactive—decide what you are going to blog about this week, then execute.

Steph: What is the most common pitfall new bloggers generally fall into?

Bob: Not having a blogging plan. A blogging plan is very much like a business or marketing plan: it answers why you are here, what are you doing and why anyone will care. Not having the answers to those questions will doom a blog.

Steph: If you knew what you know now when you first started, what's the one biggest tip you'd give yourself today?

Bob: Beware of and be prepared for blogger's blight—the strange affliction when your blogging dries up and you just don't feel you have anything to write about. Every blogger I know of, except Scoble, has come down with this malaise, as have I.

Steph: What repels you the most from a blog (animations, in your face advertising, etc.)?

Bob: Advertising in excess of the value of the blog.

Steph: Do you make any direct money from your blog through advertising, product placements, etc.?

Bob: Nope. None of my blogs currently exist for that purpose. Instead, they've brought me sales, consulting engagements and various opportunities worth far more than advertising would have brought in.

Steph: What is your best monetization method (Ads, affiliate marketing, etc.)?

Bob: The only monetization I do is Amazon Affiliates—I figure if I am helping my readers by talking with them about a book, they won't mind if I pick up a little pocket money in the process.

Steph: Do you find you get more from direct monetization of your blog or from opportunities that come because of the existence of your blog?

Bob: Opportunities by far, but then again, my blogs exist because I want to talk about, and converse with others, about those subjects, not sell eyeballs.

Steph: Thank you for taking this interview Bob.

Chapter 11

Dan Lyons

The Secret Diaries of Steve Jobs

(http://fakesteve.blogspot.com)

Dan Lyons has been in journalism for 25 years, with the last 20 covering the high tech industry. He began at PC Week and then moved on to various other trade magazines. Dan is now at Forbes, where he has been since 1998.

He's published three works of fiction including: "The Last Good Man" (short stories, 1993); "Dog Days" (novel, 1997); and "Options" (novel, 2007).

Steph: What makes a blog successful according to you? Is it traffic, reach, revenue, etc.?

Dan: Traffic is a big deal, obviously. But I also care about who's reading my blog. I have a great readership with lots of smart, funny people.

Steph: When did you decide you finally reached success with your blog?

Dan: I think when I had my first month when I had more than 1 million page views. That kind of blew me away.

Steph: How long does it take to become a successful blogger?

Dan: It took me exactly one year to hit the 1 million page view mark. I think you have to be patient and keep building the audience and keep writing even when it seems that the traffic is not growing.

Steph: Who do you think are the most successful bloggers on the internet today?

Dan: Andrew Sullivan (**http://andrewsullivan.theatlantic.com/**) is the best and most successful blogger, in my opinion. I also like Ryan Block of Engadget (**http://www.Engadget.com/**) and Brian Lam of Gizmodo (**http://Gizmodo.com/**).

Steph: Which five blogs do you regularly read?

Dan:

Andrew Sullivan (**http://andrewsullivan.theatlantic.com**)

Engadget (**http://www.Engadget.com**)

Gizmodo (**http://Gizmodo.com**).

Groklaw (**http://www.Groklaw.net**)

Cult of Mac (**http://cultofmac.com**)

Steph: Which websites would you recommend for any new bloggers starting to blog?

Dan: Read Andrew Sullivan. It's a great mix of serious essays and funny stuff.

Steph: Which book(s) would you recommend for new bloggers (these can range from marketing books, blogging books, etc.)?

Dan: No idea. I didn't read any. Maybe the Robert Scoble book (Naked Conversations) just for ideas on what NOT to do.

Steph: What is your most successful blog post ever?

Dan: I wrote a post on the day iPhone shipped—June 29, 2007 (**http://fakesteve.blogspot.com/2007/06/june-29-2007-day-world-changed.html**). It managed to be both funny and smart, if I do say so myself. Was widely linked and passed around, even mentioned as some of the best stuff written about iPhone anywhere.

Steph: What's your biggest tip on writing a successful blog post?

Dan: Write about something you care about. Don't censor yourself. Let it rip. Write from your heart.

Steph: How important do you think are the headlines of your blog articles?

Dan: Headlines are very important. I put a lot of work into them.

Steph: Do you spend any money and time on marketing?

Dan: No.

Steph: What are your quick and short five best tips for blogging?

Dan:

Only do it if you feel like you can't NOT do it.

Be passionate.

Write quickly and don't edit too much.

Post frequently. At least five a day.

Steph: What is the most common pitfall new bloggers generally fall into?

Dan: Writing about their own boring lives. Who cares? Write about something else.

Steph: If you knew what you know now when you first started, what's the one biggest tip you'd give yourself today?

Dan: Volume matters. Post frequently.

Steph: What repels you the most from a blog (animations, in your face advertising, etc.)?

Dan: Boring writing.

Steph: Do you make any direct money from your blog through advertising, product placements, etc.?

Dan: I get paid by Forbes and they go sell ads to run on my blog.

Steph: What's your most interesting story related to your blog and blogging experience?

Dan: I was blogging anonymously and hadn't told anyone at Forbes (my employer) that I was doing it. One day the publisher of Forbes wrote to me and, not knowing who I was, asked me if I wanted to come work at Forbes.

Steph: What's the one biggest opportunity that came to you because of your blog?

Dan: I've published a book based on my blog. It's called "Options: The Secret Life of Steve Jobs."

Steph: Thank you Dan for your time and taking this interview.

Chapter 12

Dane Carlson

Business Opportunities Weblog

http://www.Business-Opportunities.biz

Dane Carlson's Business Opportunities Weblog is a premier blog of ideas and opportunities for small business entrepreneurs and is one of the most widely read business blogs. In over ten thousand posts since 2001, author Dane Carlson has proven the notion that "ideas are cheap," and pushed hundreds of inventors, entrepreneurs and small scale capitalists towards their dream of owning and running their own business.

His website is currently ranked #12 (as of 12/21/2007) on the Technorati list of most popular blogs by citation.

Steph: What makes a blog successful according to you? Is it traffic, reach, revenue, etc.?

Dane: Reach and revenue go hand in hand. Every niche has some way to make it pay, whether it's through direct monetization via advertising, or indirectly by generating offline business.

Steph: When did you decide you finally reached success with your blog?

Dane: For me, success is a target, not a destination. At one point, my definition of success was one hundred regular readers. Then it was $5 a day in advertising revenue.

Today my definition of success is half a million RSS subscribers.

Steph: How long does it take to become a successful blogger?

Dane: Since success is a personal target, it depends on your goals. Give yourself six months on the low side, though.

Steph: Who do you think are the most successful bloggers on the internet today?

Dane: I was going to write my own list, but Forbes 2007 Web Celeb 25 is a great one (**http://www.forbes.com/2007/12/18/internet-fame-celebrity-tech-cx_de_07web celeb_1218land.html**)

Steph: Which five blogs do you regularly read?

Dane:

43Folders (**http://www.43folders.com**)

BoingBoing (**http://www.boingboing.net**)

DumbLittleMan (**http://www.dumblittleman.com**)

Marginal Revolution (**http://www.marginalrevolution.com**)

YosemiteBlog (**http://www.yosemiteblog.com**)

Steph: Which websites would you recommend for any new bloggers starting to blog?

Dane: Darren Rowse's Problogger (**http://www.problogger.net**), definitely. But more importantly, every single blog you can find in your niche. It doesn't matter if they publish once a month or eighteen times a day, you need to read them all.

Steph: Which book(s) would you recommend for new bloggers (these can range from marketing books, blogging books, etc.)?

Dane: I highly recommend the Cluetrain Manifesto. Don't bother reading most of the how to make money online books. By the time they're published, they're outdated.

Steph: What is your most successful blog post ever?

Dane: How Much is Your Blog Worth? (**http://www.business-opportunities.biz/projects/ how-much-is-your-blog-worth/**)

Steph: What's your biggest tip on writing a successful blog post?

Dane: Always include a link to something else. It doesn't matter if you're the smartest and wittiest writer in the world, the web is about interlinking. Link to something that backs up your argument. Link to contrarian views. Link to related subjects. Link, link, link!

Steph: What's your best advice in regards to content and writing for bloggers?

Dane: Post often.

Steph: How important do you think are the headlines of your blog articles?

Dane: People are lazy, and if you don't write good headlines, they won't bother to read your posts.

Personally, I use headlines to editorialize about the content of the blog post.

Steph: Do you spend any money and time on marketing?

Dane: No money, directly. Time, definitely.

Steph: What are your main methods of marketing your blog?

Dane: I network with other bloggers in my niche. I also write content for print publications and try to stay on Google's good side.

Never turn down an offer to have your content used elsewhere.

Steph: Which marketing tactic has surprised you the most in terms of its effectiveness?

Dane: http://www.business-opportunities.biz/projects/how-much-is-your-blog-worth/

Steph: What are your quick and short five best tips for blogging?

Dane:

Post often.

Stay on topic.

Don't apologize for not posting.

Post often!

Post often!

Steph: What is the most common pitfall new bloggers generally fall into?

Dane: Not posting and then apologizing for not posting.

Steph: If you knew what you know now when you first started, what's the one biggest tip you'd give yourself today?

Dane: I'd have chosen a shorter URL.

Steph: What repels you the most from a blog (animations, in your face advertising, etc.)?

Dane: No about page or contact information.

Steph: Do you make any direct money from your blog through advertising, product placements, etc.?

Dane: Yes, via advertising.

Steph: What is your best monetization method (Ads, affiliate marketing, etc.)?

Dane: Direct ad sales.

Steph: Do you find you get more from direct monetization of your blog or from opportunities that come because of the existence of your blog?

Dane: Most of my revenue is generated directly via ad sales, but I also generate revenue indirectly because of my blogs. I often do consulting, both for bloggers on blogging and small business entrepreneurs.

Steph: Thank you for taking this interview Dane.

Chapter 13

David Armano

Logic + Emotion

http://darmano.typepad.com/

David is currently the VP of Experience Design for the digital agency Critical Mass. He has over 14 years experience in the creative field with the majority of his time spent in digital marketing + experience design. An active thought leader in the industry, David authors the popular Logic + Emotion blog currently featured in the top tier of the "Power 150" as ranked by Ad Age. David's writing and visual thinking have been included in Forrester, Brandweek, The Boston Globe and landed him in BusinessWeek on several occasions including their "Best of 2006".

Steph: What makes a blog successful according to you? Is it traffic, reach, revenue, etc.?

David: In a word—influence. Influence is the most important way I can think to gauge a blog. It's not easy to measure influence, but popularity has something to do with it. The broader a blog's reach, the more influence it has. The more people a blog influences, the more successful it is. It's not about size—you can influence people in niche groups.

Steph: When did you decide you finally reached success with your blog?

David: Having it featured in the print version of BusinessWeek. Here's one of the few magazines that I admire and actually read and there's my blog—in full color! At that point, I felt I had crossed into a different league.

Steph: How long does it take to become a successful blogger?

David: That's like asking how long should you wait until you get married. It's different for everyone. It took me just under a year to get some serious traction—but that's rare. It could take many years. Or you could be blogging for 20 years and never reach the goal of "breaking through" to the audience you want. It's something that requires passion.

Steph: Who do you think are the most successful bloggers on the internet today?

David: As far as size goes, you've got Seth Godin (http://sethgodin.typepad.com/), Steve Rubel (http://www.micropersuasion.com/), Guy Kawasaki (http://blog.guykawasaki.com/) and Robert Scoble (http://scobleizer.com/). All have HUGE followings. Personally—I've been influenced by Bruce Nussbaum (http://www.businessweek.com/innovate/NussbaumOnDesign/), Kathy Sierra (http://headrush.typepad.com/), and I enjoy reading industry blogs such as the Adaptive Path blog (http://www.adaptivepath.com/blog/) and Putting People First (http://www.experientia.com/blog/).

Steph: Which five blogs do you regularly read?

David:

Nussbaum on Design (http://www.businessweek.com/innovate/NussbaumOnDesign/)

Adaptive Path (http://www.adaptivepath.com/blog/)

Micro Persuasion (http://www.micropersuasion.com/)

Web Strategist (http://jeremiahthewebprophet.blogspot.com/)

Putting People First (http://www.experientia.com/blog/)

Steph: Which websites would you recommend for any new bloggers starting to blog?

David:

Techno Marketer (http://technomarketer.typepad.com/)

Boing Boing (http://boingboing.net/)

Mashable (http://mashable.com/)

Steph: Which book(s) would you recommend for new bloggers (these can range from marketing books, blogging books, etc.)?

David: Made To Stick

Steph: What is your most successful blog post ever?

David: Creativity 2.E (http://darmano.typepad.com/logic_emotion/2006/06/creativity_2e.html)

Steph: What's your biggest tip on writing a successful blog post?

David: Write something that people will want to talk about. Do something that others are not. Make each post memorable.

Steph: What's your best advice in regards to content and writing for bloggers?

David: State your opinions. Don't try to write like a journalist. Do something different. Use visuals. Let your voice come through in the writing. Write in conversational tone vs. formal. Be true to your personal brand and if you don't know what that is—figure it out.

Steph: How important do you think are the headlines of your blog articles?

David: Fairly important, but not as important as the content. Best to write headlines that are both enticing and informative.

Steph: Do you spend any money and time on marketing?

David: No money spent except on Typepad. I don't market except through being myself and participating. I probably spend about 15-20 hours a week on Twitter, blogs and participating in general.

Steph: What are your main methods of marketing your blog?

David: I'll promote links on Twitter and Facebook, but the best marketing is the content. That's where I spend most of my time.

Steph: Which marketing tactic has surprised you the most in terms of its effectiveness?

David: The visuals. People love my visuals and want them for themselves. It's both my product, content and advertising. People take my visuals and distribute them on the Web. This eventually creates a bigger audience for me as most people can find their way to the source of the visual which is my blog.

Steph: What are your quick and short five best tips for blogging?

David:

Find your voice

Do something different

Be true to your brand

Provide value

Only write what makes you happy

Steph: What is the most common pitfall new bloggers generally fall into?

David: Self doubt will kill you. When you've got people commenting on your stuff or calling you out or challenging you—you have to be prepared to guard yourself from being something that isn't you. You must be yourself first, as imperfect and flawed as that may be. You won't make everyone happy. Most successful blogs are polarizing—people either love them or could care less. The worst blogs are bland, generic and have nothing original to offer. Doubting yourself is the first step down the path of boring.

Steph: If you knew what you know now when you first started, what's the one biggest tip you'd give yourself today?

David: Have an idea where you want the whole thing to end up. When I first started blogging I had no idea where I wanted it to go and went with where it took me. Now I'm a bit more strategic. I'm blogging to build credibility in the industry and to make my job more rewarding and enjoyable. I also like using it to help the company who employs me. I have a lot of freedom because of the blog. I would have established a vision for where I wanted to take it earlier.

Steph: What repels you the most from a blog (animations, in your face advertising, etc.)?

David: Bad Content, bad design and over-promotion. And also a lack of personality.

Steph: Do you make any direct money from your blog through advertising, product placements, etc.?

David: No

Steph: What is your best monetization method (Ads, affiliate marketing, etc.)?

David: My monetization is indirect. I get lots of professional opportunities.

Steph: Do you find you get more from direct monetization of your blog or from opportunities that come because of the existence of your blog?

David: I get invited to speak at places. If I were on my own, I could make a business of that.

Steph: What's your most interesting story related to your blog and blogging experience?

David: I once wrote a post that was only a sentence long and included a visual. I asked my readers to write the post for me based on the visual. The comments were amazing! Take a look for yourself. (**http://darmano.typepad.com/logic_emotion/2007/04/whats_the_story.html**).

Steph: What's the one biggest opportunity that came to you because of your blog?

David: I wrote a very popular article for BusinessWeek called "It's the Conversation Economy Stupid". I was invited to write the article because of the blog. It was a great experience—I got to work with an excellent editor and write in a very different way than blogging. It was pretty cool.

Steph: Any other comments or thoughts you'd like to share?

David: Yes. Everything I know about blogging is in this slideshow (**http://www.slideshare.net/darmano/conversation-by-design**)

Steph: Thank you David for taking this interview.

Chapter 14

David Seah

http://www.DavidSeah.com

David Seah originally studied computer engineering and computer graphics design. He eventually moved over to the professional video game industry working with the Internet and freelancing as a New Media designer/developer for a few small companies in the greater Boston area.

David then started blogging in 2004, to figure out what truly interested him and what his career path should really be. Which is when he discovered that sharing his experiences in his own words was the missing piece that eluded him in his career. And because of this discovery he flipped his priorities. Today his goal is to meet competent, conscientious, and self-empowered people like himself, which he does through collaboration and community building. He reports his experiences on his blog, and through the creation of various productivity tools such as The Printable CEO.

Steph: What makes a blog successful according to you? Is it traffic, reach, revenue, etc.?

David: Ultimately, a blog is successful when it connects people together in a way that creates opportunity and change. That generally means reaching and influencing just a handful of the right people that WANT to create that opportunity with you.

Steph: When did you decide you finally reached success with your blog?

David: I'd say early 2007 or so. I had been blogging long enough to see that it wasn't a fluke, and that the blog was doing a good job of representing myself to the world authentically, which has lead to other interesting opportunities. I am meeting fascinating people.

Steph: How long does it take to become a successful blogger?

David: If you're measuring success by traffic, then not that long if you can maintain the blogging rhythm and post compelling original content. This increases your Google footprint. After that, it's a matter of getting noticed by the larger sites, which will drive readers to you. If you write good content that is unique, they will find you. The rate of growth is then determined by the size of the demographic, your ability to write compelling original chunks of content every day, ease of accessing the chunks, and the perceived utility of your writing.

Steph: Who do you think are the most successful bloggers on the internet today?

David: I don't really follow these kinds of trends, as I don't chase after this kind of success. One person that comes to mind, though, is Virginia De Bolt (**http://www.webteacher.ws**), who I imagine would be the first to say she is not as glamorous as the A-Listers, but through blogging rediscovered her sense of purpose in a niche that embraces her. It's this kind of personal success—-connecting people with the right people—-that I consider the most important.

Steph: Which five blogs do you regularly read?

David: I actually don't read any blogs regularly...I'm quite busy these days, and when I have time to do blog-related stuff I am generally creating a new article. When I have time to surf, I'll check out the blogs of my "online council" of like-minded bloggers to see what they've been up to.

Steph: Which websites would you recommend for any new bloggers starting to blog?

David: I would tell them to check out the member sites (both past and present) that belong to the 9rules Network (**http://9rules.com**). I've been a member for quite some time, and what is particularly interesting about the group is that we're all committed to creating a better web site experience. Browse them. Find ones that appeal to you. It's helpful to have some kind of role model to follow.

Steph: Which book(s) would you recommend for new bloggers (these can range from marketing books, blogging books, etc.)?

David: No specific titles come to mind. I would just tell them to get into the habit of writing their experiences in a way that makes sense to people who don't know you or your subject; that's writing 101. Next, suck it up and put it online. For the "how do I... " technical questions, I'd probably just tell them to check out ProBlogger (**http://www.ProbBlogger.com**) or something.

Steph: What is your most successful blog post ever?

David: In terms of establishing thought leadership: The original Printable CEO Concrete Goals Tracker article, which put me on the map and started the entire chain of subsequent tools (**http://davidseah.com/blog/the-printable-ceo/**).

In terms of traffic: The Healing Power of Water, which got dug and sent about 100K visitors to me (**http://davidseah.com/blog/the-healing-power-of-water/**).

In terms of getting me recognized by a lot of cool people in the web development industry: FYI, I am Not Dave Shea (**http://davidseah.com/blog/fyi-i-am-not-dave-shea**).

Steph: What's your biggest tip on writing a successful blog post?

David: Get to the point in the first sentence, or hook 'em via some other means.

Steph: What's your best advice in regards to content and writing for bloggers?

David: Provide something useful to someone that hasn't been said before, something that people can APPLY to themselves. And don't worry about appealing to everyone; just appeal to yourself first.

Steph: How important do you think are the headlines of your blog articles?

David: Headlines give people an idea of what they're in for, so they're very important. I try to write them so they pique curiosity while also being search-engine friendly.

Steph: Do you spend any money and time on marketing?

David: No money. I do spend time on putting content out in several areas, which is in essence marketing.

Steph: What are your main methods of marketing your blog?

David: Word of Mouth, which gets me linked on other blogs, which drives first-time visitors, which result in subscriptions or bookmarks, which ultimately drives page rank.

Steph: Which marketing tactic has surprised you the most in terms of its effectiveness?

David: Word of Mouth.

Steph: What are your quick and short five best tips for blogging?

David:

Make good, original content.

Be a real person with your own opinion, but don't mistake opinion for content.

Stand behind your words.

Write constantly and consistently.

Talk to your audience in your comment area.

Steph: What is the most common pitfall new bloggers generally fall into?

David: Mistaking content for reporting about what other bloggers are writing about instead of adding something NEW to the blogosphere.

Steph: If you knew what you know now when you first started, what's the one biggest tip you'd give yourself today?

David: Nothing actually comes to mind; the blogging experience was one of exploration and empowerment of my own process, so it was very natural and unburdened with any expectations.

Steph: What repels you the most from a blog (animations, in your face advertising, etc.)?

David: Obvious commercialization.

Steph: Do you make any direct money from your blog through advertising, product placements, etc.?

David: I have some AdSense revenue, enough to perhaps cover my hosting costs. My blog is a platform, not a revenue generator in its own right.

Steph: What is your best monetization method (Ads, affiliate marketing, etc.)?

David: I haven't monetized my blog. I may create a separate web site for direct monetization of my writing, which is not the same as my blogging.

Steph: Do you find you get more from direct monetization of your blog or from opportunities that come because of the existence of your blog?

David: Opportunities, definitely, are the greatest benefit from my blog.

Steph: Thank you for the interview David.

Chapter 15

Derek Semmler

http://dereksemmler.com/

Derek is an average person in his early 30's working as a Senior Software Engineer who's doing his best to provide for his family and enjoy life along the way. His family is number one in his life, although there are times when his wife might argue that blogging has taken over that spot. Outside of spending time with his family and working on his blogs you'll likely find him on his Harley enjoying the open road.

There are three blogs where you will find Derek sharing his thoughts and opinions:

—Dad Balance (http://emomsathome.com/dad-balance) is about work life balance from a dad's perspective

—My New Choice (http://www.mynewchoice.com/) is about personal finance, eliminating debt, and money management

—Derek Semmler dot com (http://dereksemmler.com) is about life, blogging, motorcycles and just about everything else

Steph: What makes a blog successful according to you? Is it traffic, reach, revenue, etc.?

Derek: Ultimately, I believe that a blog is successful when the author has a passion for the topic of the blog and has demonstrated the ability to regularly publish content for more than six months.

It is possible, maybe even feasible, to define success by traffic, revenue, or any other measurable metric. But when you consider the number of blogs that are started each day and the fact that many of them are abandoned before they are sixty days old, I believe anyone that loves to blog and does so consistently is a success.

Steph: When did you decide you finally reached success with your blog?

Derek: I'll let you know when I get there. Personally, I would have to say that I reached success on the day that I published my very first post. Too many people sit and talk about starting a blog or making money from a blog, yet they never take action. There are many goals that I have yet to accomplish but none of them would even be possible had I not made that first post.

Steph: How long does it take to become a successful blogger?

Derek: That really depends on how you define success. If you want to be a blogger that can make thousands of dollars each month, you should be prepared for it to take a considerable amount of time. If you want to share your passion for a given topic with other people, you can become successful in a much shorter period of time. The important thing is to define what success means to you and then measure yourself against that definition.

Steph: Who do you think are the most successful bloggers on the internet today?

Derek: When thinking of the most successful bloggers, I tend to narrow my focus to those that I read regularly such as Darren Rowse (**http://www.ProBlogger.com**), Shoemoney (**http://www.ShoeMoney.com**), John Chow (**http://www.JohnChow.com**), and Brian Clark. But there are so many bloggers that have done a masterful job of building their brand and achieving success that I could likely give you a list of 100+ names and still leave out a considerable number of successful bloggers.

Steph: Which five blogs do you regularly read?

Derek: While I could easily include a list of very well known blogs such as Problogger, DoshDosh, or Shoemoney, I want to mention a handful of blogs that I enjoy reading regularly but may be a little less mainstream.

Consumerism Commentary (**http://www.ConsumerismCommentary.com**)

Riley Central (**http://rileycentral.net/wordpress/**)

Beyond the Rhetoric (**http://btr.michaelkwan.com/**)

Leo Chiang DOT COM (**http://www.leochiang.com/**)

MsDanielle (**http://www.msdanielle.com/**)

Steph: Which websites would you recommend for any new bloggers starting to blog?

Derek: There are so many great sites that I could recommend but the one site that is a must read for any blogger is Problogger. Darren has a feature titled Best of Problogger that will teach a new blogger many valuable lessons and the archives contain many more nuggets of wisdom. Just be careful not to spend so much time reading that you forget to work on your blog.

Steph: Which book(s) would you recommend for new bloggers (these can range from marketing books, blogging books, etc.)?

Derek: There is so much information available on the Interweb that I am not sure new bloggers need to rush out and buy (or get from the library) books to get started. If I had to recommend a book to new bloggers, I would probably point them in the direction of the SEO Book by Aaron Wall as it is an outstanding resource to help you learn how to build a more successful blog.

Steph: What is your most successful blog post ever?

Derek: In terms of pure traffic, I would have to say that my post about the exploding CD (**http://dereksemmler.com/2007/07/18/pictures-aftermath-of-exploding-cd/**) is the most successful with over 28,000 page views. That would be followed closely by a recent post about a rather humorous typo on Yahoo! News (**http://dereksemmler.com/2007/11/15/yahoo-news-mentions-starbucks-ass-hairs/**) with over 14,000 page views. But one of the posts that I feel is my most successful in terms of the message and what it has meant to me was my post about being a better husband (**http://dereksemmler.com/2007/06/25/being-a-better-husband/**).

Steph: What's your biggest tip on writing a successful blog post?

Derek: I'm not sure that it can be boiled down to one biggest tip but I would certainly stress the importance to write with opinion and personality. There are so many blogs out there that you need to do something to set yourself apart. Readers come to your blog for more than just the cold, hard facts—they want to know what you think and feel as well.

Steph: What's your best advice in regards to content and writing for bloggers?

Derek: Be yourself and let your voice be heard. It is tempting to try and blog about topics that you think will bring in the money or score big on the social media sites. However, when you are not blogging about something that is of interest to you and that you are passionate about, you will struggle to write quality posts that other people can connect to in some way.

Steph: How important do you think are the headlines of your blog articles?

Derek: Some might say that the headlines are the most important aspect of your blog articles, as that is what likely determines whether someone stops to read your article or not. In terms of social media, I would agree that the quality of the headline is critical. But if you put a killer headline on a garbage article, you will bring in a bunch of readers but they will likely only visit your blog that one time. So while the headline is very important, don't sacrifice on the quality of the blog post itself just to get a great headline.

Steph: Do you spend any money and time on marketing?

Derek: I've spent much more time than money on marketing my blog. The one area that I have spent money is on a monthly membership to a personal finance news aggregrator, which rewards members with highlighted entries in their feed as well as a premium listing on their blogroll.

The time that I spend on marketing is primarily spent on doing my best to become an active member of other blog communities, including other personal blogs as well as popular social media sites. For the blogger on a budget, this can be a great way to market your own blogs. As you demonstrate your value to the community on other blogs, people will naturally be interested in what you have to say and follow your links over to your blog.

Steph: What are your main methods of marketing your blog?

Derek: As I just mentioned, I would say that my main method of marketing my blog is active participation on other blogs. The easiest way to participate on other blogs is via the comments. Try to engage the author, as well as the other readers, with quality comments and you will begin to build a rapport that will likely translate to new readers at your own blog.

Other methods of marketing your blog can include writing guest posts for other blogs, publishing guest posts from other authors, including a signature line on all of your emails and/or forum posts, or being active on social media sites. The possibilities are nearly endless so just try to get out there and plant the seeds for future growth.

Steph: Which marketing tactic has surprised you the most in terms of its effectiveness?

Derek: For a new blog, I really think that one of the most effective things that you can do is to respond to the comments that readers leave on your site and return the favor by commenting on the blogs that you read. People enjoy it when they know that their comments are appreciated and it will make them feel more a part of the community.

Steph: What are your quick and short five best tips for blogging?

Derek:

Listen to your readers, there is a wealth of knowledge in their comments and it will help build a true sense of community.

Don't obsess about your blog stats, I know it is fun to check how you are doing but limit it to once or twice per week instead of once every five minutes.

When you see that someone has visited your blog, take the time to check out their blog and share a few comments.

Do not force a post, some bloggers feel that they must maintain a set schedule of posts per day or week and will force a lackluster post just to meet that quota—post when you have something to say.

Be genuine, write from the heart, and always stand behind your word as nothing will ruin you as a blogger quicker than a reputation as a fake or cheat.

Steph: What is the most common pitfall new bloggers generally fall into?

Derek: The most common pitfall seems to be a combination of burnout and unrealistic expectations. Many new bloggers think they can start publishing a few posts and they will be on their way to earning money from their blog. In the beginning, they may be posting multiple times per day as the excitement about their blog is fresh. As the days become weeks and the blogger has only earned $0.42 from AdSense, they begin to question what they are doing and they realize that they cannot maintain their current pace of posts. Eventually they lose steam and the blog falls into the pile of abandoned blogs, never to be heard from again.

Steph: If you knew what you know now when you first started, what's the one biggest tip you'd give yourself today?

Derek: I'm going to take a slogan from one of the most well known companies in our time, just do it. Don't spend so much time worrying that everything about your blog has to be perfect before you get started. Let your blog be a living creature that you build and nurture over time. The important thing is to start writing great content and building a sense of community.

Steph: What repels you the most from a blog (animations, in your face advertising, etc.)?

Derek: General websites that repel me are the ones that are entirely built using Flash. But with blogs, I really don't think anything repels me more than just a lack of updated content and/or content that does not interest me.

Steph: Do you make any direct money from your blog through advertising, product placements, etc.?

Derek: Yes, I do make money from my blogs. When I started blogging, I was guilty of the trap that many new bloggers fall into and that was thinking that using Google AdSense was the one and only source of income. As I have learned more about making money with my blogs, I have experimented with a variety of tools and resources to help me earn money. Do your best to avoid relying on only one source of income and never stop experimenting to see what works well for your blogs.

Steph: What is your best monetization method (Ads, affiliate marketing, etc.)?

Derek: The best monetization method that I have been using would have to be private ad sales, although that was not the case from day one. As your blog grows, you will likely find that the best monetization method will change as well.

Steph: Do you find you get more from direct monetization of your blog or from opportunities that come because of the existence of your blog?

Derek: At this point, I would have to say that direct monetization has brought me more.

Steph: What's your most interesting story related to your blog and blogging experience?

Derek: On my personal blog, I published a post that included pictures of what happens when a CD explodes inside your DVD drive (**http://dereksemmler.com/2007/07/18/pictures-aftermath-of-exploding-cd/**). This post brought my first experience with making the front page of Digg (**http://www.Digg.com**) and the volume of traffic was very exciting.

Not only that but I got a taste of how far a simple blog post can reach, as I was contacted by a representative of Dell who wanted to send me a free replacement DVD drive.

Steph: What's the one biggest opportunity that came to you because of your blog?

Derek: Within the last few months, I was presented with an opportunity to become an author at Wendy Piersall's eMoms at Home blog (**http://www.emomsathome.com/**) writing about work life balance from a dad's perspective. This has been such an exciting opportunity for me to write about a topic that is very close to my heart and it would not have been possible had I never started blogging.

Steph: Any other comments or thoughts you'd like to share?

Derek: Work hard, be honest, and have fun.

Chapter 16

Dharmesh Shaw

On Startups: A Community for Entrepreneurs

http://www.OnStartups.com

Dharmesh is a software entrepreneur and currently the co-founder and Chief Software Architect of HubSpot (http://www.HubSpot.com), a software company building a revolutionary software platform for Internet Marketing. HubSpot is his third software startup.

Dharmesh is a technologist, more specifically, a software developer. He's built and shipped approximately ten commercial software products across his various startups. He still programs as it keeps him in touch with reality and makes him a better entrepreneur. Plus, he enjoys it.

Prior to founding HubSpot, Dharmesh founded Pyramid Digital Solutions, an enterprise software company in the financial services sector. Bootstrapped with less than $10,000 in capital, Pyramid went on to demonstrate exceptional growth and was a three-time recipient of the Inc. 500 award. Pyramid Digital Solutions was acquired in August 2005 by SunGard Business Systems.

Since the sale of Pyramid, he has been an active member of the entrepreneurial community in the Boston area and has made several angel investments in early-stage technology companies. Dharmesh has recently graduated from MIT with an M.S. degree. As part of his graduate work, he wrote a thesis focused on software startups. Dharmesh also has a B.S. in Computer Science from the University of Alabama in Birmingham (UAB).

Steph: What makes a blog successful according to you? Is it traffic, reach, revenue, etc.?

Dharmesh: The most important two numbers I track are the number of subscribers to the blog (via RSS and email) and the daily unique visitors. This gives me a sense for how many people the content is reaching.

Steph: When did you decide you finally reached success with your blog?

Dharmesh: I'm not sure I'm there yet! I don't think it is binary (i.e. you don't wake up one day and say "yesterday, the blog was not successful. Today it is." Having said that, the big milestones for the blog , and what signaled to me that it might become popular, was when there were large spikes in traffic. These spikes occurred when I was linked to by one of the A-list bloggers or made the front page of one of the social content sites (like Digg.com or Reddit.com).

Steph: How long does it take to become a successful blogger?

Dharmesh: For OnStartups.com, it took about 6 months before there was steady traffic and the site started becoming reasonably popular. A lot depends on the topic being written about, the talent and determination of the blogger. Though it took me 6 months, my guess is really good bloggers could likely create reasonable traffic and visibility in just a couple of months.

Steph: Who do you think are the most successful bloggers on the internet today?

Dharmesh: This is a tough one, because a lot depends on how you define success. The bloggers I admire most are those that built a following through their blogging efforts—and weren't already widely known before that. For example, I love the blogs of Guy Kawasaki (**http://blog.guykawasaki.com**) and Seth Godin (**http://sethgodin.typepad.com**). But, they were both famous well before they started blogging. The ones I admire most are those that weren't really famous before they started their blogs. Examples include Brian Clark (**http://www.CopyBlogger.com**), Darren Rowse (**http://www.ProBlogger.net**), Richard MacManus (**http://www.ReadWriteWeb.com**) and Joel Spolsky (**http://www.JoelOnSoftware.com**). All of these folks used their blog to build their brand and represent (in my mind) some of the best writing on the web.

Steph: Which five blogs do you regularly read?

Dharmesh: I read lots of blogs regularly (and am subscribed to 193 feeds now, after a bit of cleanup last week). The ones I follow most closely are: TechCrunch (**http://www.TechCrunch.com**), SEOmoz (**http://www.seomoz.org/blog**), VentureBeat (**http://www.VentureBeat.com**), and Xconomy (**http://www. Xconomy.com**). Disclaimer: I'm an early investor in Xconomy, hence I have a bit of a bias).

Steph: Which websites would you recommend for any new bloggers starting to blog?

Dharmesh: I'd suggest most of what you need to know about blogging you can get from: ProBlogger.net, and CopyBlogger.com.

Steph: Which book(s) would you recommend for new bloggers (these can range from marketing books, blogging books, etc.)?

Dharmesh: I like Bob Walsh's "Clear Blogging" (but that may just be because I'm in the book). I'd also recommend "The New Rules of Marketing and PR" by David Meeman Scott. This is a great overview book of how marketing has fundamentally changed. [Disclaimer: David is on the advisory board of my startup, HubSpot].

Steph: What is your most successful blog post ever?

Dharmesh: I actually write actively for two blogs: OnStartups.com (about startups) and Blog.HubSpot.com (about internet marketing). The most successful article on my startup blog was "Hindsight 2.0: Lessons From A Failed Web 2.0 Startup" (**http://onstartups.com/home/tabid/3339/bid/115/Hindsight-2-0-Lessons-From-A-Failed-Web-2-0-Startup.aspx**) which has been viewed over 56,000 times. The most successful blog post on Blog.HubSpot.com was "12 Tips To Search Google Like An Expert" (**http://blog.hubspot.com/blog/tabid/ 6307/bid/1264/12-Quick-Tips-To-Search-Google-Like-An-Expert.aspx**) with over 107,000 views.

Steph: What's your biggest tip on writing a successful blog post?

Dharmesh: Have an opinion, take risks and always, always, always think about your readers.

Steph: What's your best advice in regards to content and writing for bloggers?

Dharmesh: People like short articles better than long ones, and bullet points more than paragraphs. We live in an impatient society. If you want to build a popular blog you should face this reality. You can write long, academic and deeply analytical articles, but it takes a lot more talent for that kind of blog to become popular.

Steph: How important do you think are the headlines of your blog articles?

Dharmesh: Extremely important. Particularly in the early days when you're just getting started. When nobody knows who you are, and your blog is not a recognized brand, the headline is your only chance to pull readers in. Doesn't matter how great your content is if nobody reads it. Once I have an idea for a blog article, I usually write the headline first.

Steph: Do you spend any money and time on marketing?

Dharmesh: I don't spend much "hard cash" on marketing. However, my blog runs on custom software that is part of HubSpot (my startup). So, in a sense I am investing in marketing by way of building the software that powers the blog. But, I don't do much direct advertising or other promotion (except as a tool to learn about how those things work).

Steph: What are your main methods of marketing your blog?

Dharmesh: The social media sites (Digg, StumbleUpon, etc.), search engine optimization and the blogosphere (participating in other people's blogs by leaving comments). Of these, the SEO investment I've made pays the highest dividends. 40% of my traffic comes from search engines now and the number continues to steadily increase.

Steph: Which marketing tactic has surprised you the most in terms of its effectiveness?

Dharmesh: I'm amazed at how effective StumbleUpon is at driving traffic over the long-term. Digg is nice for big spikes in traffic, but it is very binary (if you don't make the front page, you get almost zero traffic). But, StumbleUpon will send some modest traffic for a modestly successful article. That's good, because it's hard to make the Digg front page.

Steph: What are your quick and short five best tips for blogging?

Dharmesh:

Start! (most of the would be great bloggers have not started a blog. You could be one of them)

Write better by reading better.

Emulate the masters.

Think of your audience.

Have fun!

Steph: What is the most common pitfall new bloggers generally fall into?

Dharmesh: The most common is never getting started or abandoning too early because things don't take off. In the early days, you need to be consistent and be patient. The second is not owning your own domain. Do NOT put your blog on something.wordpress.com or something.blogger.com.

Personal Offer: If you're reading this, and are still not convinced that you need your own domain, track me down and send me an email. I'll send you $10 to pay for your first year of domain registration. Offer expires Jan 1, 2009. Quantities limited (let's say to the first 1,000).

Steph: If you knew what you know now when you first started, what's the one biggest tip you'd give yourself today?

Dharmesh: I would tell my former self to stop procrastinating and have gotten started sooner.

Steph: What repels you the most from a blog (animations, in your face advertising, etc.)?

Dharmesh: Blogs that are hard to read repel me the most. I don't mind ads as long as they don't detract too much from my consumption of the content.

Steph: Do you make any direct money from your blog through advertising, product placements, etc.?

Dharmesh: I am not monetizing the blog currently (other than to run small experiments and learn). I took all of the proceeds of 2007 from the blog and donated them to charity. Will likely do the same again next year.

Steph: What is your best monetization method (Ads, affiliate marketing, etc.)?

Dharmesh: Technically, the fixed block ads are the most valuable, but right now, I'm only advertising my own startup so no direct cash gets generated. The second most profitable vehicle is Amazon Associates (I maintain a suggested reading list page).

Steph: Do you find you get more from direct monetization of your blog or from opportunities that come because of the existence of your blog?

Dharmesh: Hands-down, the value for me is not direct monetization but from the people I come into contact with via the blog and the credibility it builds. A number of the folks I have recruited for my startup originally found me through my blog.

Steph: What's your most interesting story related to your blog and blogging experience?

Dharmesh: My most interesting experiences are when I meet random people that make reference to an article I wrote (but they don't know that I was the author). The article that gets this the most is my "Google As Dictator" article (**http://blog.hubspot.com/blog/tabid/6307/bid/1318/Google-As-Dictator-5-Most-Devious-Things-It-Could-Do-If-It-Were-Evil.aspx**). People still bring that article up in conversation and are surprised when I tell them I wrote it.

Steph: What's the one biggest opportunity that came to you because of your blog?

Dharmesh: Not to sound immodest, but I'm at a stage where I'm no longer really seeking big "opportunities" (I'm happily married and have a fast-growing startup). I already have more opportunities than I know how to deal with.

Steph: Any other comments or thoughts you'd like to share?

Dharmesh: I think blogging for business or pleasure is an immensely powerful thing. As more and more people connect online, I think they are going to start seeking targeted content about topics they care about. Everyone should try blogging, because everyone has something to say that somebody somewhere cares about.

Chapter 17

Eric Sink

Eric.Weblog()

http://www.EricSink.com

Eric is the founder of SourceGear, which sells version control tools for software developers. In October 2002, SourceGear was named one of the fastest growing companies in the nation by Inc. magazine.

Eric has a B.S. in Computer Science from the University of Illinois at Urbana-Champaign. However, these days he mostly works in marketing, although he is also a software developer. The title on his business card states "Software Craftsman" which is quite fitting.

Prior to founding SourceGear, Eric was at Spyglass (now part of OpenTV) for about five years. His role there was as Project Lead for the browser team. They built the original versions of the browser you now know as "Internet Explorer."

He also founded the AbiWord project and was responsible for much of the original design and implementation of that word processor.

Steph: What makes a blog successful according to you? Is it traffic, reach, revenue, etc.?

Eric: I guess I'd just say that I consider a blog to be successful if it has achieved the goals of its author. That seems so obvious that it seems like I'm ducking the question. Still, I know blogs with thousands of readers that aren't successful yet, and I know blogs with 2 readers that are achieving everything that is expected of them.

Steph: When did you decide you finally reached success with your blog?

Eric: No matter how you define success, it comes in plateaus. Each plateau represents a sense of achievement, but it also represents a place where the next climb is tougher.

Am I successful now? Yes, I suppose I'm standing on a plateau which allows me to look down at a lot of achievements in my past. When did I get here? I'm not sure. At some point I noticed that when I go to industry events there are a lot of people coming up to talk to me. That didn't happen before I was blogging.

Steph: How long does it take to become a successful blogger?

Eric: The time varies so much that any answer would be incorrect. I'll just say this: Some things are not under your control. Persistence is.

Steph: Who do you think are the most successful bloggers on the internet today?

Eric:

Joel Spolsky (**http://www.JoelOnSoftware.com/**)

Guy Kawasaki (**http://blog.guykawasaki.com/**)

Scott Adams (**http://dilbertblog.typepad.com/**)

Paul Graham (**http://www.PaulGraham.com/**)

Seth Godin (**http://sethgodin.typepad.com/**)

Steph: Which five blogs do you regularly read?

Eric: My RSS reader says I have 96 feeds and you only asked for 5. I always read the 5 listed above, so I'll just name 5 more of my favorites:

Charles Petzold (**http://www.charlespetzold.com/**)

Julie Lerman (**http://www.thedatafarm.com/blog/**)

Larry O'Brien (**http://www.knowing.net/**)

Miguel de Icaza (**http://tirania.org/blog/**)

Scott Hanselman (**http://www.hanselman.com/blog/**)

Steph: Which websites would you recommend for any new bloggers starting to blog?

Eric: A new blogger should start by reading at least a hundred other blogs for a month. After all that, if you still think you have something new to say, then start writing.

Steph: Which book(s) would you recommend for new bloggers (these can range from marketing books, blogging books, etc.)?

Eric: Oh I don't know. I've never read any of the blogging books, but I always hear good things about Clear Blogging.

Among the marketing classics, I recommend Positioning, Crossing the Chasm and The 22 Immutable Laws of Marketing.

But mostly I think bloggers write well if they are well-read in a lot of different things. Reading stuff that is unrelated to blogging or business is likely to be just as helpful as most anything else. Here are a few of my favorites:

The Count of Monte Cristo

Pride and Prejudice

The "Prey" novels by John Sandford

Steph: What is your most successful blog post ever?

Eric: Tough call. I'm guessing Career Calculus (**http://www.ericsink.com/Career_Calculus.html**) is probably the most popular thing I have written. Either that or my series of article on Source Control (**http://www.ericsink.com/scm/source_control.html**).

Steph: What's your biggest tip on writing a successful blog post?

Eric: If your writing is funny, nobody will notice that it's content-free.

Steph: What's your best advice in regards to content and writing for bloggers?

Eric: You've heard the old saying where the guy apologizes for writing a long letter because he didn't have time to write a short one? This is SO true.

Good writing is tight. Your final draft should probably 25–33 percent shorter than your first one.

Steph: How important do you think are the headlines of your blog articles?

Eric: Very important. I really should do a better job writing headlines for my posts, but I don't. :-)

Steph: Do you spend any money and time on marketing?

Eric: For my blog? No.

Steph: What are your main methods of marketing your blog?

Eric: My blog /is/ marketing. If I marketed my blog, then I would be marketing my marketing. Then I would want to market the marketing of my marketing. I wouldn't know where to stop.

Steph: Which marketing tactic has surprised you the most in terms of its effectiveness?

Eric: Google AdWords, but that's becoming less and less true over time.

Steph: What are your quick and short five best tips for blogging?

Eric:

Make your writing enjoyable.

Write short entries often, not long entries seldom.

Good writing takes time. If it takes you less than a morning to write an entry and make it really polished, then it's probably not worth posting.

Don't be gratuitously provocative just to get readers.

Nobody wants to look at a screen full of long paragraphs. Break things up. Use subheadings, bulleted lists, and graphics.

Steph: What is the most common pitfall new bloggers generally fall into?

Eric: Most people don't realize how much endurance is necessary. They start a blog with the lofty goal of writing a 500 word entry every day. A month later they've written 4 entries and they feel like quitting.

Steph: If you knew what you know now when you first started, what's the one biggest tip you'd give yourself today?

Eric: For me, blogging is a secondary activity. My primary job is running a software company. What I didn't know back when I started was that in 2007, lots of people will be blogging as their primary activity and making a living doing it. I don't think it would have changed my approach, but I certainly would have found it interesting to know.

Steph: What repels you the most from a blog (animations, in your face advertising, etc.)?

Eric: When I first see a blog, I very quickly form an opinion about one key question: Which is more important to this blog? Revenue or readers? Blogs which value revenue or readers just don't interest me very much.

Steph: Do you make any direct money from your blog through advertising, product placements, etc.?

Eric: I get an Amazon Affiliate gift certificate every month. Not one of those certificates has been enough to buy a new video game.

Steph: Do you find you get more from direct monetization of your blog or from opportunities that come because of the existence of your blog?

Eric: The latter.

Steph: What's your most interesting story related to your blog and blogging experience?

Eric: In a very small sphere of the blogging world, I am a mini-celebrity. People see me as some kind of software marketing wizard who has the answer to their problems.

In my personal sphere, I'm just a normal guy. My wife sees me as the guy who forgets to take the trash can out to the street about half the time.

I think it's funny when these two spheres collide. My sister recently told me a story about a social function she attended. (Background: My sister is not in the software field, and her married name is not Sink.)

She and her husband got stuck at a table with a bunch of geeks who started talking about software. One of them was apparently a big fan of my blog. He said, "I'd really like to meet Eric Sink sometime. I bet he's a really interesting guy."

Unable to resist the opportunity, my sister said, "You know, I've met that guy, and he's really not that interesting at all." :-)

Steph: What's the one biggest opportunity that came to you because of your blog?

Eric: The publishing of my book. This wasn't a big money-maker, but the opportunity to become a published author has been nice.

Steph: Any other comments or thoughts you'd like to share?

Eric: Good blogging is hard. In part this is because good writing is hard, but I think blogging is even tougher. It's a special kind of writing, and the economic incentives are even more difficult than traditional writing.

I guess I think my blog is successful, but that's mostly because my primary goal is to write for the joy of writing.

Personally, I think if I had set out to write a blog with a certain goal for revenue or readership, I probably would not have succeeded. That's one of the things that make blogging tough. The success criteria tend to become an obstacle to doing it well.

Chapter 18

Ian Landsman

http://www.UserScape.com/blog/

Ian Landsman is the founder of UserScape, a great help desk web based software solution sold internationally.

Ian was successful pretty early on with UserScape. In just a few months he was able to get a good number of links to his new product and that enabled him to launch it with a large beta group. That very solid beta group was a very big part of HelpSpot's early success and really got things rolling for him. In the first month after HelpSpot went on sale the company sold enough licenses to cover all the startup costs they'd accumulated over the 8 months of development.

Ian is also the author of his own blog which has a strong following with many software developers. He shares his experiences and thoughts on software development and running a business through his blog.

Steph: How long does it take to become a successful blogger?

Ian: If you have reasonable goals there's no reason you can't have success within a few months.

Steph: Who do you think are the most successful bloggers on the internet today?

Ian: Of course this is really dependent on the type of blogger I read and relate to. I'd say Joel Spolsky (**http://www.JoelOnSoftware.com**), Eric Sink (**http://www.EricSink.com**), and Dave Winer (**http://www.scripting.com/**) are tops for me.

Steph: Which five blogs do you regularly read?

Ian:

Dave Winer (**http://www.scripting.com/**)

Jason Calacanis (**http://www.calacanis.com/**)

Eric Sink (**http://www.EricSink.com**)

Joel Spolsky (**http://www.JoelOnSoftware.com**)

Patrick McKenzie (**http://microisvjournal.wordpress.com/**)

Steph: Which websites would you recommend for any new bloggers starting to blog?

Ian: There weren't many websites I found which really helped get me rolling with blogging. I think the most important thing is to read a lot of blogs, be focused on what you want to write about and comment on a lot of blogs. Blogging is definitely best learned by doing it and interacting with the blogging community.

Steph: Which book(s) would you recommend for new bloggers (these can range from marketing books, blogging books, etc.)?

Ian: I like Clear Blogging by Bob Walsh (of course I'm in it!). I think Seth Godin's Purple Cow book has a lot of great marketing advice which is relevant to blogging as well.

Steph: What is your most successful blog post ever?

Ian: That's a tough one. There's a few which have been very popular, but I'd say my post on creating a business logo (**http://www.userscape.com/blog/index.php/site/comments/creating_a_business_logo**) is number one. It's actually a really simple post about how I worked with my designer (Mike Rohde) on creating logo's for UserScape and HelpSpot. I think it really clicked with people because my designer sketches everything out first and I included screenshots of the entire process so it was very visual.

The post is almost two years old, but it's still number one on Google when you search for creating a business logo.

Steph: What's your biggest tip on writing a successful blog post?

Ian: Know your readers. It's easy to tell when you write a post that your readers don't respond to because you won't get any comments. You want to try and write for your readers, that's how you'll have the most success.

Steph: What's your best advice in regards to content and writing for bloggers?

Ian: Well I can tell you that you don't have to be a great writer. It helps of course, but I'm not and I've done fine. If your ideas and content are compelling the rest will take care of itself.

Steph: How important do you think are the headlines of your blog articles?

Ian: Headlines are very important for a few reasons. Just like a newspaper, the headline is what grabs your readers. Just as important, the headline is what search engines will index on and what searches will click on. So if you want your posts to be highly viewed choosing the right headline is critical.

Steph: Do you spend any money and time on marketing?

Ian: I don't spend any money on marketing. In the beginning I did spend a lot of time on marketing though. I spent hours reading other blogs and commenting on their posts. Commenting is a key factor in gaining readers. I still do more commenting than actually writing for my blog, it's really my favorite aspect of blogging.

Steph: What are your main methods of marketing your blog?

Ian: The only real marketing is comments and links from other blogs.

Steph: Which marketing tactic has surprised you the most in terms of its effectiveness?

Ian: None really. It's not surprising that the most time consuming tactic (making relevant comments on other blogs) generates the best results.

Steph: What are your quick and short five best tips for blogging?

Ian:

Write often

Comment on relevant blogs

Link to others often

Write on topic

Use full content RSS feeds

Steph: What is the most common pitfall new bloggers generally fall into?

Ian: Certainly it's that they don't realize how much work it is and they fade out. They start a blog and do a few posts. They get no comments and no readers on those posts so they stop. They don't realize that it's a marathon not a sprint.

Steph: If you knew what you know now when you first started, what's the one biggest tip you'd give yourself today?

Ian: I probably would have written a bit more about the help desk industry and not just about creating a startup, but I'm happy with how things turned out so I can't complain.

Steph: What repels you the most from a blog (animations, in your face advertising, etc.)?

Ian: Definitely advertising. I think what people don't understand is that making $20/month on some AdWords is nothing compared to what you could be doing by using that space to promote yourself or your own products. I only have a small advertisement for HelpSpot (my own product) on my blog and nothing else. Some single posts from my blog have generated $20,000+ in revenue. That's far more than that post could ever generate from AdWords.

Steph: Do you make any direct money from your blog through advertising, product placements, etc.?

Ian: Only by promoting my own product, no other outside advertising. This revenue has been very significant.

Steph: What is your best monetization method (Ads, affiliate marketing, etc.)?

Ian: The best posts are ones that relate to your target market and that include the links you're trying to monetize in the content itself.

Steph: Do you find you get more from direct monetization of your blog or from opportunities that come because of the existence of your blog?

Ian: Overall the opportunities created by the blog are more significant than direct monetization though that's been very good as well. Specifically, the inbound linking and search engine ranking of my product have been infinitely improved by blogging and this indirect effect has had a substantial impact on my business.

Steph: What's your most interesting story related to your blog and blogging experience?

Ian: One interesting aspect of having a semi-popular blog is that friends and family think you're famous. Often my blog will come up for searches unrelated directly to me. It's always funny when families bring this up and are shocked that I'm in Google.

Steph: What's the one biggest opportunity that came to you because of your blog?

Ian: The biggest direct opportunity was to be part of several books on business and blogging. These are opportunities I never would have had otherwise.

Steph: Thank you Ian for the interview.

Chapter 19

James & Alex

Google SightSeeing

http://GoogleSightSeeing.com

James and Alex are brothers and the authors of Googlesightseeing.com. They are both professional web developers by day and planetary explorers by night. Although often assumed to be American, they actually come from the beautiful city of Edinburgh, Scotland. Alex has a degree in Graphic Design (his talents have previously won him a trip to New York), and is currently a digital media developer. James has a degree in Computer Science and is employed as a senior web developer. James' talents have won him awards for web development and innovation at the BBC Radio 1 National Student Radio Awards.

When Google launched their revolutionary online map service, Google Maps in April 2005, they immediately began excitedly scanning the photos for recognizable landmarks. The site featured stunning photos of large parts of the Americas taken using a combination of satellite and aerial photography. After spending an evening tracking down more sights and sharing them with their friends, the brothers decided that they would share their discoveries with a wider audience and so the Google Sightseeing blog was born.

Google Sightseeing has continued to expand and grow, offering readers new and exciting places to visit each day from the comfort of their chair with Google Earth or Google Maps. They have since been covered in numerous online and print publications including The Guardian, Newsweek, TIME magazine's "50 coolest websites of the year", San Francisco Chronicle, LA Times, New York Post, Wired, as well as TV coverage on BBC News 24, and FOX 26.

In 2006 they released a photo book based on the website which was published as "Not In the Guide Book" in Europe and "Off the Map" in the United States. Each image was accompanied with a humorous and insightful description of the, often very bizarre, sight to be seen. Reviews of the book were extremely positive and a second volume is under consideration.

Steph: What makes a blog successful according to you? Is it traffic, reach, revenue, etc.?

James & Alex: It's all about the numbers! Along with every other blogger out there, we're pretty much obsessed with seeing how many people visit, read, comment on and discuss our website. One of the best things about success is reading other people's blog posts about our site—it's a great way of getting feedback on what we do, and gives us a fantastic feeling of pride to read the things that people say about us to their own readers.

Steph: When did you decide you finally reached success with your blog?

James & Alex: Straight away—because very soon after starting the blog hundreds of people bookmarked Google Sightseeing on del.icio.us (this was before the days of Digg). At this point we realized just how many people were also interested in what we were doing, and so we considered it a success, even at that very early stage! After that huge initial interest, we knew we could make it work if we dedicated ourselves to the project.

Steph: How long does it take to become a successful blogger?

James & Alex: From our experiences less than a day, but we would assume that is not the usual answer! We rode a wave of interest in Google Maps and Earth.

Of course the site was ripped off and copied extensively but we think because we've always involved the readers and invited comment and opinions our site has stood the test of time while our imitators and rippers off have faded away through lack of interest.

Steph: Who do you think are the most successful bloggers on the internet today?

James & Alex: People define success differently—for some it's all about revenue—so it's difficult to say who has achieved the most of their own personal blogging goals. Sometimes it seems that once the most obviously successful blogs reach critical mass, somebody buys them up or the people that started the blog give way to newer fresher faces. This means that the most "successful" bloggers don't actually seem to do much blogging...which is a shame.

Steph: Which five blogs do you regularly read?

James & Alex:

Google LatLong (**http://google-latlong.blogspot.com/**)

Google Maps Mania (**http://googlemapsmania.blogspot.com/**)

Strange Maps (**http://strangemaps.wordpress.com/**)

Ogle Earth (**http://www.ogleearth.com/**)

Google Earth Blog (**http://www.gearthblog.com**)

Steph: Which websites would you recommend for any new bloggers starting to blog?

James & Alex: Those which are relevant to your field!

Steph: Which book(s) would you recommend for new bloggers (these can range from marketing books, blogging books, etc.)?

James & Alex: Well, our own book "Not In the Guide Book" / "Off the Map" obviously.

Steph: What is your most successful blog post ever?

James & Alex: Without a doubt, our most popular post is the "Top 10 Naked People on Google Earth" (**http://googlesightseeing.com/2006/11/28/top-10-naked-people-on-google-earth/**) which, over a year after posting, still accounts for 12% of the total traffic to our site.

The story actually starts with a different post from September 2006, the "Topless Sunbather" (**http://googlesightseeing.com/2006/09/19/topless-sunbathing/**). Suggested by one of our readers, the image of a building in the Netherlands appeared to show a very fuzzy image of a person sunbathing in the privacy of their roof terrace. Because of the low resolution of the image it was impossible to tell the gender of this person, or even if they were truly "topless", but they were certainly slightly undressed so we posted onto Google Sightseeing as a humorous entry.

We didn't anticipate the interest that the post would generate, and once it was on the front page of popular news site Digg.com, our server crashed under the load. Despite this, the entry was seen by over 60,000 people in one day!

It was obvious to us that the mash-up of potential nudity with a popular technology like Google Earth was a winning combination for Digg readers, so we considered the possibility of adding another popular topic on Digg—the top 10.

And so we unashamedly wrote the ultimate Digg post—the Top 10 Naked People on Google Earth, and it of course was a complete success with Digg readers. Who'd have thought so many people wanted to see pixilated potential nudity?

Steph: What's your biggest tip on writing a successful blog post?

James & Alex: You have got to be really really interested in your subject. You can't expect other people to be interested if you aren't interested enough to keep it up to date. If you get bored with it shows.

Steph: What's your best advice in regards to content and writing for bloggers?

James & Alex: Get your apostrophes right! Of course writing for the web is not like writing school essays, but wilful misspellings and atrocious grammar just make your stuff unreadable, and put people off—as do mad fonts and repeated punctuation like this!!!!!!!!! and the overuse of smileys and totally UNNECCESSARY capitalization and all the usual crimes against the language you see on poor quality web pages every day.

Steph: How important do you think are the headlines of your blog articles?

James & Alex: Very—people read this stuff in their feed reader, and with such information overload, it's hard to make people click the title to get them to read your story! It's a tricky art, and it really depends on your market how you write your titles. Listen to your readers and hopefully you'll come up with the winning formula. It's tempting to write article titles in one of the proven ways that attracts Digg readers, but this doesn't help your blog build readers in the long term.

Steph: Do you spend any money and time on marketing?

James & Alex: We don't do any marketing- we're too busy doing our blog, which is our marketing!

Steph: What are your quick and short five best tips for blogging?

James & Alex:

Listen to your readers; don't patronize, antagonize or con them.

Spell hceck your work!

Write original stories—you can't get away with any kind of plagiarism these days.

Have a sense of humour.

Steph: What is the most common pitfall new bloggers generally fall into?

James & Alex: Thinking that just because they're interested in their gerbil / their job / their gym shoes everyone else is going to be too—other people might be, but only if it's written well.

Steph: If you knew what you know now when you first started, what's the one biggest tip you'd give yourself today?

James & Alex: Don't think you're going to make a million blogging.

Steph: Do you make any direct money from your blog through advertising, product placements, etc.?

James & Alex: Google Ads is our friend and we aren't sure our nearest and dearest would be at all happy about the hours we spend away from them working on the site if we weren't able to point to small regular income as a result.

Steph: What is your best monetization method (Ads, affiliate marketing, etc.)?

James & Alex: Ads without a doubt.

Steph: Do you find you get more from direct monetization of your blog or from opportunities that come because of the existence of your blog?

James & Alex: In the short term in direct but other opportunities do arise in the long term, although you might not realize it at the time.

Steph: What's the one biggest opportunity that came to you because of your blog?

James & Alex: Writing the blog led to writing our book, which was a fantastically rewarding experience not just financially but because of the opportunities it gave us to go on TV and radio to talk about it.

Steph: Thank you James and Alex for the interview.

Chapter 20

J.D. Roth

Get Rich Slowly

http://getrichslowly.org/blog/

J.D. is a self-described middle-aged geek born and raised in rural Oregon. He studied psychology and writing in college, but when he graduated he went to work for the family business as a box salesman. Though he hated the job, he couldn't leave because he found himself deep in debt. During the 1990s, he dug himself even deeper into debt, buying computer games, books, and comics.

He's been writing for the web since 1994, and has had some sort of web journal since 1997. J.D. started his first blog in 2001. For years, he just wrote for family and friends. But in 2005 he created a post that summarized all the stuff he had learned from personal finance books. This received attention from all corners of the internet, and made him realize there was a hunger for information like this. So in April 2006, J.D. started Get Rich Slowly where he writes about personal finance and how to get more out of life.

Steph: What makes a blog successful according to you? Is it traffic, reach, revenue, etc.?

J.D.: I run several blogs. Each blog has a different measure of success. My personal blog is successful if it keeps my friends and family informed and entertained. I don't need a lot of traffic there, but to maintain a connection to the people I know. Similarly, at my animal intelligence site (**http://www.animalintelligence.org/**), I measure success by how many stories I can find and share, not by traffic.

At Get Rich Slowly, however, things are different. My number one measure for success is feedback from readers: are people finding the content useful and relevant? But I'm much more interested in traffic numbers there. In particular, I try to build my subscription numbers. RSS readers are important to me. I'm less interested in page views and unique visitors.

Revenue is a secondary concern for me. Don't get me wrong: the money is nice, but it's not my top priority. I am grateful that I'm earning enough from blogging to allow me to quit my day job, but I'd still blog even if I didn't.

Steph: When did you decide you finally reached success with your blog?

J.D.: I don't know. I've been writing various blogs for nearly seven years (and "on-line journals" for even longer). For most of that time, I've dwelled in relative anonymity. I guess it's only recently that I've begun to think of myself as a successful blogger, and that's only because doing this now can support me full-time.

Steph: How long does it take to become a successful blogger?

J.D.: There's no one answer to this. Some bloggers achieve success over night. Some bloggers never do. The answer, of course, depends on your definition of success. For most people, however, it takes months or years.

Steph: Who do you think are the most successful bloggers on the internet today?

J.D.: I have no idea.

Steph: Which five blogs do you regularly read?

J.D.: The only blogs I read regularly are those of my family and friends. That said, I do read some blogs more than others.

I read Darren Rowse's Problogger to stay up-to-date on blogging topics. (**http://www.Problogger.com**)

I read Mike Sterling's Progressive Ruin to stay up-to-date on comic books. (**http://www.progressiveruin.com/**)

I read Mac Rumors to stay up-to-date on Macintosh topics. (**http://www.macrumors.com/**)

I read kottke.org because I always have (and always will). (**http://kottke.org/**)

I read Scott Adams' Dilbert Blog because I find him funny, intelligent, and engaging. (**http://dilbertblog.typepad.com/**)

I try to read the sites in my niche at least once a week, but I don't always have time for that.

Steph: Which websites would you recommend for any new bloggers starting to blog?

J.D.: Steve Pavlina's article on how to make money from your blog is excellent. I think it's the best single piece of information on this subject (**http://www.stevepavlina.com/blog/2006/05/how-to-make-money-from-your-blog/**)

There are only two actual web sites, however, that I think most bloggers need to read: Problogger (**http://www.problogger.net**) and Copyblogger (**http://www.copyblogger.com**). These sites consistently provide excellent information.

Steph: Which book(s) would you recommend for new bloggers (these can range from marketing books, blogging books, etc.)?

J.D.: I strongly believe that the skill most bloggers—including myself—need to improve is writing. I don't think bloggers need to read marketing books or blogging books. They need to read books about writing. I recommend the following:

On Writing Well by William Zinsser

On Writing by Stephen King

The Elements of Style by Strunk & White

One of my readers recently pointed me to "Weinberg on Writing: The Fieldstone Method" by Gerald Weinberg, but I haven't had a chance to read it yet.

Two non-writing books that I also believe are useful:

The War of Art by Steven Pressfield, which deals with procrastination and fear, etc.

The Incredible Secret Money Machine by Don Lancaster, which is a late-seventies manual for starting a small business. When I re-read this recently, I was amazed at how much of the advice applied to my situation as a "pro" blogger.

But marketing books? I can't imagine how a marketing book would be useful to me as a blogger.

Steph: What is your most successful blog post ever?

J.D.: How do you measure success? I've had posts with high bursts of traffic:

Twenty mp3s of Great Songs from 1901-1920 (**http://www.foldedspace.org/weblog/2006/06/in_the_good_old_summertime.html**)

Building a Personal Finance Library: 25 of the Best Books About Money (**http://www.getrichslowly.org/blog/2007/03/07/building-a-personal-finance-library-25-of-the-best-books-about-money/**)

And I've had posts with a "long tail", constant steady traffic for months (or years):

Which Online High-Yield Savings Account is Best? (**http://www.getrichslowly.org/blog/2007/03/21/which-online-high-yield-savings-account-is-best/**)

adhesive capsulitis (**http://www.foldedspace.org/weblog/2002/09/adhesive_capsulitis.html**)

But to me, the most successful posts are those that help people change their lives. I know this sounds Pollyanna, but it's true. People tell me that posts like these help them turn their financial situation around:

How to Start a Roth IRA (and Where to Do It) (**http://www.getrichslowly.org/blog/2007/06/07/how-to-start-a-roth-ira-and-where-to-do-it/**)

How to Get Out of Debt (**http://www.getrichslowly.org/blog/2006/11/16/how-to-get-out-of-debt-2/**)

If I had to choose one post as my "most successful", however, I'd have to pick "The Power of Yes: A Simple Way to Get More Out of Life" (**http://www.getrichslowly.org/blog/2007/06/13/the-power-of-yes-a-simple-way-to-get-more-out-of-life/**)

This was an intensely personal article describing a technique I'd been using to draw myself out, to become more engaged with the world. It took me months to write. I was scared to post it even, afraid of possible negative reaction. (I posted it at Get Rich Slowly, and it's not really about personal finance.) Instead, it enjoyed all three measures of success: a burst of high traffic, sustained traffic over the long-term, and, most importantly, it has helped people change their lives. People write every week to thank me for sharing that. To me, that's success.

Steph: What's your biggest tip on writing a successful blog post?

J.D.: Be honest. Write from your experience, but make the information accessible to readers. Don't turn out a post filled with dull statistics or filled with dry term-paper paragraphs. Imagine that *you* are a reader coming to your site for the first time. If you were to find this post, would you stick around?

Not all blog posts can be winners, of course, but each post should be the best it can possibly be. It should contain useful information (or entertaining information, depending on the blog). It should be well-written. It should encourage the reader to action.

Steph: What's your best advice in regards to content and writing for bloggers?

J.D.: Content and writing are two different things. I address writing elsewhere in this interview. As for content: be interesting. Try to avoid the "echo chamber". Every blog niche has one. Among personal finance blogs, one person will write on a subject ("how to save money on cheese!"), and then there'll be a ripple effect as other people respond ("my top 5 ways to save money on cheese!", "why processed cheese is better than the real stuff", "top 5 blog posts about cheese"). Some of this is natural—there will always be article you want to respond to—but too much of it is lame.

To use one example: John Chow has carved out a very successful niche for himself. He has a good blog and some devoted readers. But many of his readers create blogs that seem to be solely responses to John Chow. Don't do that. Let John Chow write about John Chow. You write about yourself and what is important to you. If you don't know a damn thing about making money on the internet, then don't write about it. Write about your paper airplane collection instead. I'd rather read a good blog about paper airplanes (or saving money on cheese) than to read yet another person responding to John Chow.

Steph: How important do you think are the headlines of your blog articles?

J.D.: Ah, this is a fine question. I think headlines are very important. I think there's an art and a science to writing good headlines. I don't have much skill in this area, though. I know enough to avoid "cute" headlines (though sometimes I forget), but I don't know how to turn a mundane headline ("The Pros and Cons of an Interest-Only Mortgage") into something more interesting. Sometimes I get lucky, but most of the time this is a weak spot in my blogging.

Steph: Do you spend any money and time on marketing?

J.D.: No.

Steph: What are your main methods of marketing your blog?

J.D.: I build and maintain relationships with other bloggers. I accept and contribute guest posts. But I don't do these things with marketing in mind. I do them because I *like* to and because they foster community. Marketing is a side-effect.

Steph: What are your quick and short five best tips for blogging?

J.D.:

Take a writing class at your local community college.

Don't start a blog because you want to make money. Start a blog because you're passionate about the subject. I don't know *any* bloggers who have achieved success without being totally into their subject.

Write daily, even if you don't post daily. Get in the habit of writing.

Learn to edit yourself! I spend more time editing my material than I do actually writing it.

Don't worry about SEO. Search engine optimization does *not* make a successful blog. Writing content that people want to read makes a successful blog. (I've literally done zero SEO at Get Rich Slowly.)

Steph: What is the most common pitfall new bloggers generally fall into?

J.D.: Wanting overnight success. Readers and traffic come with time. You can't start a blog for fame and fortune. You have to start it for love. If the passion isn't there, the other things will probably never come.

Steph: If you knew what you know now when you first started, what's the one biggest tip you'd give yourself today?

J.D.: This is going to seem like a non-sequitur based on my previous answers, but...

When I started Get Rich Slowly, I just chose an out-of-the-box WordPress template. I made modifications to it as I went along. If I had any idea that this site was going to be successful, I would have been more methodical about my layout. I hate my template, but now I feel tied to it. I've done my best to bend and stretch the Connections theme to suit my needs, but I really want something more suited to my needs. I just created a custom WP theme for my personal site, though, and this will help me do the same for GRS in the future.

So, the biggest tip I'd give myself is: make sure your blog layout is the way you want it before you even start. But I don't think that's useful info for most people.

Steph: What repels you the most from a blog (animations, in your face advertising, etc.)?

J.D.: Though poor design and too much advertising can be turn-offs, there are two things that really make me wince:

Poor writing. If you can't write, then don't. Sharpen your writing skills!

Blatant money-grubbing. I'm not talking about advertising, but rampant promotion of affiliate links, etc. This stuff is fine in moderation, but if it oughtn't be the reason for your blog.

Steph: Do you make any direct money from your blog through advertising, product placements, etc.?

J.D.: Yes. I make income from all my blogs. Some generate only $5 or $10/month, but that's because I do a poor job of maintaining them. Get Rich Slowly currently produces about $5,000/month in revenue.

Steph: What is your best monetization method (Ads, affiliate marketing, etc.)?

J.D.: Adsense and FeedBurner are very close for me. This surprises many people who find FeedBurner to be a poor source of income. I have a lot of subscribers, though, and I've intentionally kept the Google ads at Get Rich Slowly understated. I have no doubt that if I wanted to be more aggressive, Adsense could earn 2-4 times what it does now.

Steph: Do you find you get more from direct monetization of your blog or from opportunities that come because of the existence of your blog?

J.D.: I haven't earned anything because of the opportunities. Not yet, anyhow.

Steph: What's the one biggest opportunity that came to you because of your blog?

J.D.: I've been contacted by several book publishers and one agent. They're interested in a Get Rich Slowly book. This is something that appeals to me, but I haven't had the time to pursue it. It's a priority for 2008, however. So, no opportunities yet, but there's one on the horizon...

Steph: Any other comments or thoughts you'd like to share?

J.D.: Blogging is a dream come true for me. Not blogging itself, but the opportunity it gives me to write everyday. I've always wanted to be a writer. I just never pictured myself writing about personal finance for the web. (I thought I'd write fantasy or science fiction novels.) Now that I'm doing it, however, I understand that this is what I'm meant to do. My whole life has been leading to this. It's awesome.

Chapter 21

Jeff Atwood

Coding Horror

http://www.CodingHorror.com

Jeff Atwood lives in Berkeley CA with his wife, two cats, and a whole lot of computers. He was weaned as a software developer on various implementations of Microsoft's BASIC in the 80's, starting with his first microcomputer, the Texas Instruments TI-99/4a. He continued on the PC with Visual Basic 3.0 and Windows 3.1 in the early 90's, although Jeff also spent significant time writing Pascal code in the first versions of Delphi. He considers himself a reasonably experienced Windows software developer with a particular interest in the human side of software development.

Computers are fascinating machines, but they're mostly a reflection of the people using them. In the art of software development, studying code isn't enough: you also have to study the people behind the software. And Jeff is definitely at the forefront of this.

His site is one of the most popular software development blogs online with about 100,000 visitors each day!

Steph: What makes a blog successful according to you? Is it traffic, reach, revenue, etc.?

Jeff: You should write selfishly, to satisfy only yourself, or you'll burn out instantly. But all writing is meant to be read. The true metric of success for any kind of writing is how many people are reading. All other success factors derive from that.

Steph: When did you decide you finally reached success with your blog?

Jeff: When I hooked up RSS and web statistics packages for the first time, I found I had accumulated a surprisingly large audience.

Steph: How long does it take to become a successful blogger?

Jeff: At least a year. Perhaps six months if you're extraordinarily good.

Steph: Who do you think are the most successful bloggers on the internet today?

Jeff: How you measure success? I tend to think of it in terms of audience, which loosely translates to impact on the world. You can only influence a very small percentage of readers, so the more you have, the more action your words will create. It's a numbers game. So by that metric, I'd say the most highly read blogs—which may have more than one author—are the most successful. I don't enjoy the gamesmanship that things like the Technorati (**http://www.Technorati.com**) top 100 and RSS reader metrics tend to cultivate, but they're as good a place as any for measuring influence.

Steph: Which five blogs do you regularly read?

Jeff: I don't have a specific list that I recommend. I hesitate to hand out blanket recommendations, I think it's better for people to explore and find things they care about rather than relying on what someone else thinks is important. The internet is a big place; it's more fun to go off road and explore rather than visiting the same places as everyone else. Just share your finds with the rest of us!

Steph: Which websites would you recommend for any new bloggers starting to blog?

Jeff: I'd say find someone who's writing you admire and try to emulate what they do.

Steph: Which book(s) would you recommend for new bloggers (these can range from marketing books, blogging books, etc.)?

Jeff: I recommend reading books specific to the field you're interested in. Honestly, so much great information is locked up in books, you could spend a year mining various books for blog topics. I suppose this is why Google and others are so hot on book scanning. Let's unlock that information and share it with the world.

Steph: What is your most successful blog post ever?

Jeff: Probably "Why Can't Programmers.. Program?" (**http://www.codinghorror.com/blog/archives/000781.html**), where I capped the comments at about 500. That one really seemed to capture people's imaginations. The odd thing is, that post was just a quick one-off on a topic I thought was marginally interesting, and it completely exploded. It's so difficult to predict what people will respond to, which is why I don't think you should try to. Just follow your interests. I will say that, based on my experience, intentionally trying to incite controversy will get you more attention. Unfortunately, not all of it will be attention that you want, but that's the price you pay. It's a dangerous game, and that's why I'd rather take up chainsaw juggling than become a political blogger.

Steph: What's your biggest tip on writing a successful blog post?

Jeff: Don't become an echo chamber or a news ticker. Put in some effort and do some original research. Synthesize something new.

Steph: What's your best advice in regards to content and writing for bloggers?

Jeff: Write down any ideas you have so you can dig them up later and piece them into a blog post as necessary. Strike while the iron is hot. Even if you don't have time to flesh it out, take enough notes so that you can "just add water" and reconstitute it later as needed. Unfortunately, that fleshing out process can be painful, depending on the topic. When I'm stuck, I stop worrying about writing an introduction or a conclusion and just start wherever I have the strongest feelings and inclination. Then I build around that. Getting started is the hardest part. Once I get going, it's easier to carry that momentum forward and write the rest of the post.

Steph: How important do you think are the headlines of your blog articles?

Jeff: Hugely important. The title is often the last thing I do. I usually put in some filler title while I'm editing, then as I get to the end of the piece, the title will reveal itself. You can usually extract some clever, zingy phrase from the post itself and transform that into the title. Do not try to start by writing a great title. You'll never get anywhere. I do know that.

Steph: Do you spend any money and time on marketing?

Jeff: None. I have been fortunate in that the marketers have come to me. Spend the lion's share of your time creating great content. The rest, miraculously, takes care of itself if you are patient. It's hard to believe, but it really is true.

Steph: What are your main methods of marketing your blog?

Jeff: Create connections. Reach out to your peers—follow what other people do and post thoughtful comments that show you're actually interested in what they're doing and saying. Because you are, right? You're a part of that community. Link to your peers liberally in your posts, even those that don't agree with you. Also try to reach outside your community regularly for other perspectives.

Steph: Which marketing tactic has surprised you the most in terms of its effectiveness?

Jeff: I find it slightly distasteful, but disclosing my RSS and page view statistics has opened doors for me. There's a certain "roar of the crowd" that people will respond to, even if they have no real respect for you or your writing. But if they see that 100,000 people read what you're writing every day, it must be good—right? Actually, no, but I suppose that's all part of the fun.

Steph: What are your quick and short five best tips for blogging?

Jeff:

Cultivate an inquisitive personality.

Learn to enjoy researching things obsessively.

Commit to a schedule and stick to it.

Start anywhere.

If something compels you to write about it, harness and ride that wave. But try to be objective, too.

Steph: What is the most common pitfall new bloggers generally fall into?

Jeff: They become an echo chamber. Most blog entries regurgitate what other people have said, or add a thin layer of commentary on top of news articles and press releases. We have the whole of human history to talk about, and most people can't get past what happened today. If everyone else is talking about it, that means you should avoid talking about it. Switch things up. Seek out uncommon sites with unique information. Dig down to original sources and read the material everyone is commenting (comments on top of comments on top of comments) endlessly on. If all you can find to talk about is what's already popular, you're not trying hard enough. Form your own opinion. Do your own research. Go out of your way to blaze a new trail and create something we haven't already seen hundreds of times before.

Steph: If you knew what you know now when you first started, what's the one biggest tip you'd give yourself today?

Jeff: Start blogging in 2000. If you trace back the truly influential bloggers, they all started extremely early. Otherwise, start immediately, and stick to a schedule. You don't get better by thinking about it or talking about it. You get better by doing it. So get going!

Steph: What repels you the most from a blog (animations, in your face advertising, etc.)?

Jeff: Lots of spelling mistakes and grammatical errors are a huge turn off. As a blogger you're basically a writer. A few mistakes every now and then are OK, but if you look like you don't care about your writing, why should we? Writing well is hard enough without people screwing up the simple mechanical parts of it. I find this difficult to forgive.

Steph: Do you make any direct money from your blog through advertising, product placements, etc.?

Jeff: I negotiate directly with advertisers to fill a fixed set of three ad slots on my blog. I also make extensive use of Amazon affiliate links where it's appropriate for the topic—mostly books.

Steph: What is your best monetization method (Ads, affiliate marketing, etc.)?

Jeff: The best possible relationship is to negotiate directly with advertisers and cut out the middlemen. It's ideal for both parties. The only thing to worry about is the perception of bias, as there's no division between the writing department and the sales department. Just be honest and up front, and your audience will generally do the same.

Steph: Do you find you get more from direct monetization of your blog or from opportunities that come because of the existence of your blog?

Jeff: It's an even mix of both. I don't solicit work through my blog, so the opportunity vector is much more indirect and hard to measure. But it's definitely there. People are much more willing to work with companies or people they've heard of. Now that blogging has become so mainstream, saying you heard about someone or something on a blog is a legitimate calling card. Strange times we live in.

Steph: What's your most interesting story related to your blog and blogging experience?

Jeff: It's amazing the people who will find you through your blog, once it's been out there long enough. I've been in contact with a number of long-lost friends and business associates through my blog. Perhaps the most unlikely was a childhood friend I barely remembered from a brief one year period living in a small southern town. I have no idea how he connected the dots and recognized me through my blog, but he did.

Steph: What's the one biggest opportunity that came to you because of your blog?

Jeff: Probably the realization that I could truly quit my job as a software engineer and become a full-time writer, if I wanted to. I have no interest in doing so, but that shocked me.

Steph: Thank you for the interview Jeff.

Chapter 22

Jeff Clavier

Jeff Clavier's Software Only

http://blog.softtechvc.com/

In May 2004 Jeff left his position of General Partner of the Reuters Greenhouse Fund, the corporate venture arm of Reuters, to start his own firm, SoftTech VC. He began investing as an angel (with his own money) in very early stage consumer internet startups in Silicon Valley. Social Media was one of his investment themes, and despite the fact that he had been a VC for over four years, he did not have the network in the early stage world, especially in the nascent Web 2.0 crowd. Starting a blog in this market made absolute sense, and Software Only was born in an evening of June 2004, the day before the BlogOn conference.

He decided on the blog title Software Only because he, an angel investor, would only back companies developing software products or services; companies with no physical moving pieces, no inventory. Within the following 2 years, he wrote over 500 posts covering the startup and the investing world, commenting on news in the technology world, announcing news about his companies, etc.

Jeff's RSS reader count during this time also grew from a small number to the current count of over 82,000. He's since been invited to write guest posts for ZDnet and a few other online properties. All in all, blogging had been extremely useful and strategic to the deal flow for his companies.

However successful Jeff has been, he also feels it had taken too much of a tax of his time. On the second birthday of his blog (which happened around his 500th post) he decided to slow down blogging and instead focus on the top 10 blogs covering the Web 2.0 industry in Netvibes. And this is what makes Jeff somewhat unique in the book. He's the only blogger in this book who's already retired from blogging. However, the bug of sharing his ideas, views and whereabouts still remains. You can sometimes find him on micro-blogging sites like Twitter, etc.

Steph: What makes a blog successful according to you? Is it traffic, reach, revenue, etc.?

Jeff: The popularity of a blog in its target market would be the measure I would use, that popularity being a function of readership and engagement. Readership is simply the number of people visiting the blog organically, through search or direct links, or subscribing to its RSS feed. Engagement is based on the number of comments per posts, and the average number of visits per readers. Whether the key metric is more readership than engagement depends on the type of blog, or the type of post.

Making serious money on a blog, through advertising or sponsorship, is reserved to the "head of the tail" where traffic and CPMs (Cost Per Impressions—usually measured in eCPM, effective cost per thousand impressions) reach minimum levels. However making money thanks to a blog, as a mean to acquire or grow visibility and exposure, absolutely works—even with modest traffic or readership levels—provided that the right audience is engaged. Even now that I only blog a few times a year, thanks to RSS, I still have a very large readership which I can address on topics that I am motivated to blog about.

Steph: What is your most successful blog post ever?

Jeff: Interestingly, most of my most successful posts were related to announcements of acquisitions of companies in the Web 2.0 space. Most recently, the announcement of the launch of my fund got a fair amount of visibility and comments. I wish that blogging platforms were doing a better job at capturing these analytics and data points.

Steph: What's your biggest tip on writing a successful blog post?

Jeff: Right size your posts in order to facilitate their consumption. An announcement without context or analysis should fit in one paragraph. A deeper analysis could take much more, but you still want to make sure to use a style that makes the piece easy to read and puts a lot of the useful information in the first few sentences. You want the teaser—the first few sentences—to be engaging to entice the reader to go further. If relevant, add a picture or a video to the post.

Link to references or other useful information. I personally don't like posts that contain too many links, but point of views vary on that matter. Tag it with the relevant terms, and trackback to the blogs that you linked to if they don't do it automatically.

Steph: What are the top five methods of marketing you'd most recommend?

Jeff:

Use proper tags and URL naming to increase indexing/discoverability of a post

If related to some recent news, figure out which post(s) might get on top of techmeme.com (**http://techmeme.com**) and write an analysis post that links to them

Post frequently about your domain(s) of expertise in order for people interested in it/them add you to their blogroll

Make sure to always mention your blog URL in any profile you fill in (LinkedIn, MySpace, Facebook, etc.) as well as your email signature and your business card

Write OP'ed pieces on popular blogs and add at least one link to a post of yours

Chapter 23

Jennette Fulda

Half of Me

http://www.PastaQueen.com

Jennette Fulda was born weighing 8 pounds 5 ounces, but eventually tipped the scales at 372 pounds before losing over 200 pounds through diet and exercise. Her book "Half-Assed: A Weight-Loss Memoir" was published by Seal Press in May 2008 and chronicles how she lost over half her weight without losing her sense of humor. She writes the popular blog, Half of Me (pastaqueen.com), which has been mentioned in the Wall Street Journal and Glamour. She also contributes articles to Capessa at Yahoo! Health, the Condé Nast health, and the fitness blog Elastic Waist. She works in Indianapolis as a web developer and writer.

Steph: What makes a blog successful according to you? Is it traffic, reach, revenue, etc.?

Jennette: It depends on the purpose of the blog. If you're blogging to make money, you're successful when you start cashing ad checks. If you're blogging to be famous, you're successful when you start getting lots of page views. If you're blogging to make the Internet love you, you're successful when people start sucking up to you.

Steph: When did you decide you finally reached success with your blog?

Jennette: I felt like a success personally when I started getting comments from people who found truth in my entries. I felt like a success professionally when I landed a book deal from my blog. And I felt like a success as an entrepreneur when I started making money off of my blog.

Steph: How long does it take to become a successful blogger?

Jennette: It depends. If you get a gig at a big blog network like Gawker, your blog can be popular and profitable from the day you launch. If you're growing your blog at home, it can take years to build a steady audience and revenue stream.

Steph: Who do you think are the most successful bloggers on the internet today?

Jennette: I admire people who are able to live off of their blogs, like Heather Armstrong at http://www. dooce.com, Jason Kottke at http://www.kottke.org or Darren Rowse at http://www.problogger.net. You can tell that they like what they do and aren't just in it for the money. Or if they are, they hide it pretty well.

Steph: Which five blogs do you regularly read?

Jennette:

Crazy Aunt Purl—She's drunk, divorced, and covered in cat hair. (http://www.crazyauntpurl.com)

Seal Press Blog—My publisher not only prints books, but blogs about women's interests. (http://www.sealpress.com/blog.php)

Jane in Progress—Scriptwriter Jane Espenson blogs about writing and what she ate for lunch (http://www.janeespenson.com/)

What's Alan Watching?—This New Jersey Star-Ledger TV blogger keeps me alerted to what is worthy of my eyeball time (http://sepinwall.blogspot.com/)

A Dress a Day—Lots of dresses! (http://www.dressaday.com/dressaday.html)

Steph: Which websites would you recommend for any new bloggers starting to blog?

Jennette:

ProBlogger—Great information on how to run a successful blog (http://www.problogger.net/)

WordPress—Dynamic blogging platform with an active development community and lots of beautiful templates (http://wordpress.org/)

Steph: Which book(s) would you recommend for new bloggers (these can range from marketing books, blogging books, etc.)?

Jennette: Half-Assed: A Weight-Loss Memoir, of course! The author started as a blogger, after all. If you want to write a book based on your blog, read other books by bloggers to see how they did it.

Steph: What is your most successful blog post ever?

Jennette: I still get comments on an entry about the weird things I used to binge on. I invited readers to post the strangest things they used to eat and I got over a hundred responses. I even learned some people ate orange juice concentrate straight out of the can like I used to. (**http://www.pastaqueen.com/halfofme/archives/2007/06/bad_habits.html**)

Steph: What's your biggest tip on writing a successful blog post?

Jennette: Invite your readers to share their own stories and advice on a topic that really engages them. Or write an article about a topic lots of people want to know about. A lot of obese people are curious as to whether they'll have loose skin when they lose weight, so I wrote an entry about that which was well received.

Steph: What's your best advice in regards to content and writing for bloggers?

Jennette: Be honest and let your personality shine through. The best bloggers are authentic. Also, use a spell-checker. It's free and it makes you look smarter.

Steph: How important do you think are the headlines of your blog articles?

Jennette: They're important for search engine optimization, but I tend to write oblique titles that act as punch lines to my entries. I like to be creative with my headlines instead of just angling for lots of hits.

Steph: Do you spend any money and time on marketing?

Jennette: I haven't spent any money, but I've spent time doing interviews that help promote my blog.

Steph: What are your main methods of marketing your blog?

Jennette: I comment on other people's blogs, but mostly because I like to and not just for marketing. I also do interviews in books about blogging.

Steph: Which marketing tactic has surprised you the most in terms of its effectiveness?

Jennette: I once gave away a free track suit I'd received from a company promoting their athletic gear. I was amazed at how many people entered or posted links on other blogs about how to enter.

Steph: What are your quick and short five best tips for blogging?

Jennette:

Blog frequently

Blog well

Set boundaries and stick to them. (Who and what will you blog about? Who and what won't you blog about?)

You have to give before you get. (If you want to generate an active community, you have to go out and be a part of that community.)

Blog because you love it.

Steph: What is the most common pitfall new bloggers generally fall into?

Jennette: They quit. Stick with it and you're more likely to see results.

Steph: If you knew what you know now when you first started, what's the one biggest tip you'd give yourself today?

Jennette: Register a domain name! I didn't have any big plans for my blog, so I just hosted it in a folder on my personal web site. Eventually the blog became so popular I let it take over my domain instead of registering a new one. At that point I had so many links coming to pastaqueen.com that if I were to move to a new domain name, my rank on search engines and blog listings would have dropped significantly.

Steph: What repels you the most from a blog (animations, in your face advertising, etc.)?

Jennette: Ugly fonts, text in multiple colors, and big chunks of text with no paragraph breaks. These things make a blog hard to read on the screen. Even if a blog is well-written, I wouldn't bother to read one that's illegible.

Steph: Do you make any direct money from your blog through advertising, product placements, etc.?

Jennette: Yes. I feel very sneaky making money off of something I would be doing anyway. I feel like I've tricked the universe somehow. I like to make money off of my passion, but my passion isn't making money.

Steph: What is your best monetization method (Ads, affiliate marketing, etc.)?

Jennette: I get the most money off of ad networks, but I make a reasonable amount from Amazon affiliate links too. People ask me for recommendations for workout DVDs or scales anyway, so I point them to products I enjoy and make a small commission. I do not use systems that generate ads from key words because I know I'd get lots of ads for diet pills. As someone who's lost a lot of weight, it would be unethical for me to promote weight-loss products I don't use. I don't want any of my visitors thinking I lost 200 pounds with pills. I could be making more money if I used those kinds of ads, but I would feel dirty about it.

Steph: Do you find you get more from direct monetization of your blog or from opportunities that come because of the existence of your blog?

Jennette: As of this writing, I've made more money from other opportunities than from my blog, but I believe my book and my blog will help each other by cross-promoting one another.

Steph: What's your most interesting story related to your blog and blogging experience?

Jennette: I got to visit the Hallmark corporation's headquarters in Kansas City, Missouri. They paid for my air fare, a night in a swanky hotel, and a huge sushi dinner. I got to tour their facilities with several other bloggers and ate M&M's with the Hallmark logo on them. I was worried they'd want me to promote something for them in return, but instead they were more interested in picking our brains and learning what blogging was all about.

Steph: What's the one biggest opportunity that came to you because of your blog?

Jennette: I got to write a book. That in turn taught me a lot about writing, marketing, and the publishing industry.

Steph: Any other comments or thoughts you'd like to share?

Jennette: Blogging has allowed me to grow as a person, meet lots of new friends, and created many opportunities. I enjoy the fact that my blog is popular and that I make money off of it, but it's important not to let too much of my self-esteem get wrapped up in its perceived success. People who say they love your blog today, can just as easily say they hate it tomorrow. You may be getting a zillion hits this year, but who knows how many people will be dropping by next year? What's really important is the feeling of self-satisfaction I get from writing and the relationships that I've formed through my blog. All the rest is just icing on the cake I'm not eating.

Chapter 24

Jennifer Perry

101 Reasons I Hate Being Fat!

http://101reasonsihatebeingfat.blogspot.com/

Jennifer Perry is in her thirties and lives in New Haven, CT. She's just completed her PhD at Yale University in molecular cellular and developmental biology.

With all of her successes, Jennifer, unfortunately feels she's got one failure, hence the inspiration of her blog: 101 Reasons I Hate Being Fat.

She can tell you that she's pretty much tried every diet possible and nothing in the past had worked for her. She's tried being really positive when approaching weight loss, and it never seemed to work for her. She just kept coming back to the idea that she simply hated being overweight.

Then she says a light bulb went off in her head and she thought "let's look at this with a negative spin", and that's when 101 Reasons I Hate Being Fat was born. It's looking at something negative like the fat and how bad it makes us feel, and poking fun at it. She turned something negative into something positive and created a blog that has a very active community. The ratio of people commenting compared to the level of traffic she gets is significant.

Steph: What makes a blog successful according to you? Is it traffic, reach, revenue, etc.?

Jennifer: Blog success for me is a numbers game—high traffic = success. I'm a scientist after all, it's all about the hard data!

Steph: When did you decide you finally reached success with your blog?

Jennifer: It's successful? Just kidding. Probably after I hit 50,000 hits, with comments flooding in about how much people liked my blog. Every month the hit rate goes up and up, it really makes me smile to know that people are reading.

Steph: How long does it take to become a successful blogger?

Jennifer: Depends on the blogger. If you advertise, maybe it comes faster. Word of mouth only (like me), might take a long time. For me, I was blogging over a year before people really started taking notice.

Steph: Who do you think are the most successful bloggers on the internet today?

Jennifer: I honestly only read blogs in my genre—weight loss. I think 'Half of Me' (**http://www.pastaqueen.com**) and 'The Amazing Adventures of Dietgirl' (**http://www.dietgirl.org/**) are the most successful diet bloggers.

Steph: Which five blogs do you regularly read?

Jennifer:

Half of Me (**http://www.pastaqueen.com**)

The Amazing Adventures of Dietgirl (**http://www.dietgirl.org/**)

Angry Fat Girlz (**http://angryfatgirlz.blogspot.com/**)

Do you have an extra large in this? (**http://largemarshmallow.blogspot.com/**)

Adventures of a born again gym bunny (**http://www.ypweightloss.blogspot.com/**)

Steph: Which websites would you recommend for any new bloggers starting to blog?

Jennifer: I'm a big fan of Blogger—super easy platform to start blogging!

Steph: Which book(s) would you recommend for new bloggers (these can range from marketing books, blogging books, etc.)?

Jennifer: Books? Bloggers read actual books? All my web info comes directly from the source—the internet. I really don't use any print media for resources.

Steph: What is your most successful blog post ever?

Jennifer: You just never know what is going to strike a nerve in your readers. For me it was a post where I documented a typical day in the life of a fat person and how much I think about food (**http://101reasonsihatebeingfat.blogspot.com/2007/08/79-thinking-about-weight-all-time.html**). I described my day thought by thought, minute by minute. For some reason people really responded and the comments flooded in!

Steph: What's your biggest tip on writing a successful blog post?

Jennifer: Write from the heart. My posts that have been the most honest have been the most successful and well liked.

Steph: What's your best advice in regards to content and writing for bloggers?

Jennifer: Again write from the heart, write what you know. People love honesty and realism. Stick with that and you'll be successful.

Steph: How important do you think are the headlines of your blog articles?

Jennifer: Very important! It's what grabs the reader and says hey this is going to be interesting. I'm all about the catchy slogans. My blog title is even catchy.

Steph: Do you spend any money and time on marketing?

Jennifer: Nope.

Steph: What are your quick and short five best tips for blogging?

Jennifer:

Write what you know

Be honest

Be funny

Be willing to make fun of yourself

Don't let your posts get too long—people get bored with long long blog posts (but I must admit I am guilty of this often—I tend to ramble, ramble, ramble... look I'm even rambling now!)

Steph: What is the most common pitfall new bloggers generally fall into?

Jennifer: Expecting a lot of blog traffic instantly, then giving up when they don't see the numbers. Like I said it took a year of blogging for me before people noticed my blog.

Steph: If you knew what you know now when you first started, what's the one biggest tip you'd give yourself today?

Jennifer: Post more. I tend to let a lot of time lag between my posts, leaving my readers waiting. I probably lose some readers just by not posting enough.

Steph: What repels you the most from a blog (animations, in your face advertising, etc.)?

Jennifer: You said it- animations, music, obnoxious ads, garish colors, difficult to navigate pages with millions of links. I like a simple blog that is easy to read and navigate. Too irritating or hard to read—I just don't read it then.

Steph: Do you make any direct money from your blog through advertising, product placements, etc.?

Jennifer: Nope. Theoretically I have a partnership with Amazon, but I have yet to earn any money.

Steph: What's your most interesting story related to your blog and blogging experience?

Jennifer: Overall I think just the fact that what I set out to do with this blog is working. I wanted something to keep me motivated to help me lose weight. People tell me I inspire them to lose weight, but what they don't realize is that it's their comments that inspire me. In the past year I have lost 65 pounds (and still losing). The goal of the blog was to lose one pound for every post. Hmmm... will I be able to lose 101 pounds once I get to the end of the list? Maybe. But the most important thing is that I am helping not only myself to lose weight, but I'm setting an example for others to follow. That feels really great!

Steph: What's the one biggest opportunity that came to you because of your blog?

Jennifer: I was asked to be on a weight loss TV show, but I wasn't able to participate because I was finishing my PhD.

Steph: Any other comments or thoughts you'd like to share?

Jennifer: A word of advice for new bloggers. If you think you might have something to say, say it! Write, write, write, write! Readers love hearing stories about people in similar situations as them. Find an audience that can relate to you and just talk to them.

Chapter 25

Jessamyn West

Librarian.net

http://www.librarian.net

Jessamyn is a library technologist living in rural Vermont. She grew up in rural Massachusetts and was drawn to librarianship because of her love to read and the idea that everyone deserves access to the information that they want and need. Jessamyn is a community moderator on MetaFilter.com. She travels around the US and the world speaking on library technology issues, particularly library 2.0 topics and the digital divide. Jessamyn runs the websites librarian.net and jessamyn.com and has been maintaining a blog of some sort for over ten years.

Steph: What makes a blog successful according to you? Is it traffic, reach, revenue, etc.?

Jessamyn: Success means having an impact, whatever you want that to be. For me it's getting dissemination for the ideas of myself and others and watching those ideas have a ripple effect through the profession.

Steph: When did you decide you finally reached success with your blog?

Jessamyn: I'm both totally satisfied and never satisfied with how successful my blog is.

Steph: How long does it take to become a successful blogger?

Jessamyn: Totally varies, again with how an individual measures success.

Steph: Who do you think are the most successful bloggers on the internet today?

Jessamyn: The ones who are using their blogs to do exactly what they want them to do. I think of the BoingBoing crew (**http://www.boingboing.net**), Matt Haughey (**http://a.wholelottanothing.org/**), the people who started Flickr (**http://www.flickr.com/**) and Vox (**http://www.vox.com/**) and the political bloggers who are finding wide audiences for their analyses.

Steph: Which five blogs do you regularly read?

Jessamyn: I read about 150 blogs regularly. These are some of my favorites.

Freedom to Tinker (**http://www.freedom-to-tinker.com/**)

Ask MetaFilter—where I also work (**http://ask.metafilter.com**)

RandomWalks (**http://www.randomwalks.com/**)

The Laboratorium (**http://laboratorium.net/**)

Rebecca's Pocket (**http://www.rebeccablood.net/**)

Steph: Which websites would you recommend for any new bloggers starting to blog?

Jessamyn: I wouldn't really. If people want to blog they are reading blogs already generally and good blogging is, to me, about finding your own voice and style. It's also about, to me, bringing the offline online.

So read books and the newspaper, go out and meet people and have those experiences inform your online writing.

Steph: Which book(s) would you recommend for new bloggers (these can range from marketing books, blogging books, etc.)?

Jessamyn: I'm fond of The Weblog Handbook (**http://www.rebeccablood.net/handbook/**)

and Social Software in Libraries, for librarians (**http://www.sociallibraries.com/**)

Steph: What is your most successful blog post ever?

Jessamyn: Well, the one that got the most comments was about the children's book that was finding itself removed from some libraries because it had the world "scrotum" in it (**http://www.librarian.net/stax/1978/scrotum/**). Although the one about me making a little movie about installing Ubuntu may be ahead of that one (**http://www.librarian.net/stax/2042/do-you-ubuntu/**).

Steph: What's your biggest tip on writing a successful blog post?

Jessamyn: I don't know, I don't think of "success" as a goal. If you want to be effective, you should write about what you care about in such a way that people will both want to read it *and* want to do something about it.

Steph: What's your best advice in regards to content and writing for bloggers?

Jessamyn: Have your own style and substance. It's easy to just repost and round-robin pass along links that other people have already been talking about and that can get you page rank and maybe readers, but having original stuff or even original takes on the same old stuff is appreciated. Also be kind or at least gentle to everyone. Grace under pressure, for the long haul, is a good ability to cultivate.

Steph: How important do you think are the headlines of your blog articles?

Jessamyn: They're important if you care about where your blog posts fall in Google or other search engines, otherwise they're just like headlines in a newspaper. They can be games and it's always sad to see people doing that.

Steph: Do you spend any money and time on marketing?

Jessamyn: No, not as such.

Steph: What are your main methods of marketing your blog?

Jessamyn: In a way, going out and commenting on other blogs is a form of marketing, but I'd be doing that anyhow. I'm always a bit freaked out by people who want to have a successful destination blog but don't go out and interact sincerely on other blogs.

Steph: Which marketing tactic has surprised you the most in terms of its effectiveness?

Jessamyn: Linkspam/linkfarm blogs. If you have a bunch of spammy crappy non-blogs that link to you or "comment" on your blog, your Technorati rank will increase even though those spammy blogs bring no new content to the web.

Steph: What are your quick and short five best tips for blogging?

Jessamyn:

Be kind.

Be original.

Be thoughtful.

Be part of a community.

Ignore bad juju in its many forms.

Steph: What is the most common pitfall new bloggers generally fall into?

Jessamyn: They link to a bunch of stuff on the web but don't link to other bloggers so no one finds out about them. They don't invest enough of themselves into something.

Steph: If you knew what you know now when you first started, what's the one biggest tip you'd give yourself today?

Jessamyn: Split the personal from the professional earlier. I have a professional and a personal blog and while I try to be human on both, I think they have different goals. That said, I'm pretty happy with how it all turned out so far.

Steph: What repels you the most from a blog (animations, in your face advertising, etc.)?

Jessamyn: Too many ads. I won't read a blog with ads in the RSS feeds.

Steph: Do you make any direct money from your blog through advertising, product placements, etc.?

Jessamyn: I have occasionally run fundraisers and used my blog to direct attention to an eBay auction to give money away. Otherwise no.

Steph: Do you find you get more from direct monetization of your blog or from opportunities that come because of the existence of your blog?

Jessamyn: I get invited to a lot of public speaking gigs and get a lot of work because of my blog.

Steph: What's the one biggest opportunity that came to you because of your blog?

Jessamyn: I recently was invited to give a keynote presentation at a library conference in Dubai, UAE which was a really interesting and eye-opening trip. I was also invited to be an "official" blogger at the Democratic National Convention in 2004.

Steph: Thank you for the interview Jessamyn.

Chapter 26

Joel Cheesman

Cheezhead

http://www.cheezhead.com

Joel Cheesman is one of the most widely-read bloggers on emerging recruitment issues in the world. He was the recipient of Recruiting.com's Best Technology Recruitment Blog for 2005 and received Best Recruiting Blog in 2007. He has been featured in Fast Company magazine and its blog under FC Reads, as well as NewsNow, Workforce Management, AIRS, Crain's Business, BusinessWeek Magazine, Resumes for Dummies and The Wall Street Journal (print addition).

Joel's blog is about how the Internet and technology are shaping human resources and how organizations can attract the talent needed to thrive in tomorrow's economy. As an employee and insider of some of America's biggest online job sites since 1997, Joel founded HRSEO to help employers and companies with recruitment.

Joel is also an evangelist of search engine optimization (SEO), Internet marketing and other emerging technologies that help employers and similar businesses drive targeted candidates to vacancies.

Steph: What makes a blog successful according to you? Is it traffic, reach, revenue, etc.?

Joel: It's mostly about the Benjamins, but personal growth and having a creative outlet are important too.

Steph: When did you decide you finally reached success with your blog?

Joel: Success is a journey. What defined success a year ago is different now. That said, I first realized success as my primary business, HRSEO, was getting more business via blog posts than anything else.

Steph: How long does it take to become a successful blogger?

Joel: I think you either have it or you don't. Time depends on the talent.

Steph: Who do you think are the most successful bloggers on the internet today?

Joel: Follow the money. Techcrunch (**http://www.techcrunch.com/**), Perez Hilton (**http://perezhilton.com/**) and the like. Success also means expanding past blogging. For example, Techcrunch is into conferences.

Steph: Which five blogs do you regularly read?

Joel: In no particular order:

Techcrunch (**http://www.techcrunch.com/**)

Marketing Pilgrim (**http://www.marketingpilgrim.com/**)

SEOmoz (**http://www.seomoz.org/**)

SEO BlackHat (**http://seoblackhat.com/**)

Seth Godin (**http://sethgodin.typepad.com/**)

Steph: Which websites would you recommend for any new bloggers starting to blog?

Joel: Wordpress.org (**http://wordpress.org/**), Performancing (**http://performancing.com/**), any top blogs in their niche

Steph: Which book(s) would you recommend for new bloggers (these can range from marketing books, blogging books, etc.)?

Joel: Purple Cow, Origin of Brands, The Dip

Steph: What is your most successful blog post ever?

Joel: I was the first to blog about Yahoo! HotJobs aggregating content from other job sites and putting it on their own (**http://cheesman.typepad.com/seo/2005/07/yahoo_ups_ante_.html**). That put me on the map.

Steph: What's your biggest tip on writing a successful blog post?

Joel: Care about what you're writing about. Passion equals interesting.

Steph: How important do you think are the headlines of your blog articles?

Joel: Very. With so much clutter and competition for attention, a bad headline means your post is D.O.A. Likewise, a good one can make the post.

Steph: Do you spend any money and time on marketing?

Joel: Of course.

Steph: What are your main methods of marketing your blog?

Joel: SEO, PPC, acquiring other blogs, public speaking, conferences, social networking

Steph: Which marketing tactic has surprised you the most in terms of its effectiveness?

Joel: Social networking (MySpace, Facebook)

Steph: What are your quick and short five best tips for blogging?

Joel:

Write a lot.

Frequency should be consistent.

Use Wordtracker's free tool to defeat writer's block (**http://freekeywords.wordtracker.com**)

Don't rely too much on one tactic (mix in podcasts and video with written word)

Be a David to a Goliath

Steph: What is the most common pitfall new bloggers generally fall into?

Joel: Expecting stardom after a couple of posts.

Steph: If you knew what you know now when you first started, what's the one biggest tip you'd give yourself today?

Joel: Start using your own domain instead of something like myblog.typepad.com.

Steph: What repels you the most from a blog (animations, in your face advertising, etc.)?

Joel: Boredom.

Steph: Do you make any direct money from your blog through advertising, product placements, etc.?

Joel: Yes.

Steph: What is your best monetization method (Ads, affiliate marketing, etc.)?

Joel: Sponsorship (**http://www.cheezhead.com/2007/01/15/cheezhead-sells-out/**)

Steph: Do you find you get more from direct monetization of your blog or from opportunities that come because of the existence of your blog?

Joel: Exterior opportunities.

Steph: What's your most interesting story related to your blog and blogging experience?

Joel: I once auctioned myself off on eBay (**http://www.cheezhead.com/2006/06/11/jobcentral-wins-auction/**)

Steph: What's the one biggest opportunity that came to you because of your blog?

Joel: The opportunity to connect with great people.

Steph: Any other comments or thoughts you'd like to share?

Joel: Nope. Gotta go blog.

Chapter 27

Jonathan Snook

Snook.ca

http://snook.ca/jonathan/

Jonathan Snook is currently a freelance web developer based in Ottawa, Canada. A Renaissance man of the Web, he has programmed in a variety of languages, both server-side and client-side. He also does web site and web application design. Jonathan worked for more than seven years with web agencies, getting to work with Fortune 500 clients. He made the leap to freelance back in January 2006.

Jonathan likes to share what he knows through speaking, writing books, writing for online magazines such as Digital Web and Sitepoint, and writing for his own popular blog at Snook.ca. He is the co-author of the acclaimed Accelerated DOM Scripting with Ajax, APIs, and Libraries and of The Art and Science of CSS.

Steph: What makes a blog successful according to you? Is it traffic, reach, revenue, etc.?

Jonathan: Success is whatever you want it to be. For me, it's about a lot of things. It's about traffic, it's about reach, and it's about revenue.

But it's also about helping others and when somebody goes out of their way to let me know that I've helped them, that's success.

Steph: When did you decide you finally reached success with your blog?

Jonathan: When people started calling me "A-list". Even then, I denied it. I didn't feel successful. Nothing had really changed in any big way. I still don't consider myself "A-list" but I do realize that I have a lot of people who follow what I write and that's an honour.

Steph: How long does it take to become a successful blogger?

Jonathan: I think that depends on how much effort you put into it. I see people behind sites like FreelanceSwitch and Smashing Magazine that pump out content that gets linked like crazy. And they do this within a relatively short amount of time. Mind you, these are collaborative sites but pull out a quality design with a few decent posts and you're well on your way.

For me, it took a while. I'm basically a turtle who took it slow and steady to win the race.

Steph: Who do you think are the most successful bloggers on the internet today?

Jonathan: I guess it depends on the qualification of success. Plenty of people have been able to parlay their blogging success into other endeavors like Cameron Moll (**http://www.cameronmoll.com/**) and Dave Shea (**http://www.mezzoblue.com/**).

Steph: Which five blogs do you regularly read?

Jonathan: Using a feed reader, I read whoever posts regularly. That's people like Simon Willison's link log (**http://simonwillison.net/**), Jeremy Keith (**http://domscripting.com/blog/**), Ajaxian (**http://ajaxian.com/**), YUIBlog (**http://yuiblog.com/**) and any number of other sites.

Steph: Which book(s) would you recommend for new bloggers (these can range from marketing books, blogging books, etc.)?

Jonathan: Building Findable Websites is coming out soon and would be a good match for the new blogger.

Steph: What is your most successful blog post ever?

Jonathan: 6 keys to understanding modern CSS-based layouts (**http://snook.ca/archives/html_and_css/six_keys_to_understanding_css_layouts/**)

Steph: What's your biggest tip on writing a successful blog post?

Jonathan: Sadly, putting together top 10 lists can bring in a lot of traffic. I feel like it's a cheap and easy ploy but it totally works.

Steph: What's your best advice in regards to content and writing for bloggers?

Jonathan: Just write what you know and what you run into. Most of all, just write. Your writing style will evolve into something that works for you and your audience.

Steph: How important do you think are the headlines of your blog articles?

Jonathan: Headlines are extremely important. They should be considered for attracting traffic and for search engine practicality. Coming up with a witty title will usually just hurt your chances of success by confusing users.

Steph: Do you spend any money and time on marketing?

Jonathan: I spend plenty of time on the blog but don't market it outside of the blogging I do day-to-day. I do some writing for other publications and link-backs help promote me and my site.

Steph: What are your main methods of marketing your blog?

Jonathan: Writing for other sites along with continuing to post on my own site helps further the promotion of the site.

Steph: Which marketing tactic has surprised you the most in terms of its effectiveness?

Jonathan: I don't think there's been one specific approach I've tried to take. I've really let the growth be organic.

Steph: What are your quick and short five best tips for blogging?

Jonathan:

Write

Read what others do.

Write more (don't stop).

Chunk your writing. Break up the page into subsections and lists. Makes the content easier to read.

Keep writing (don't stop, ever).

Steph: What is the most common pitfall new bloggers generally fall into?

Jonathan: Not writing.

Steph: If you knew what you know now when you first started, what's the one biggest tip you'd give yourself today?

Jonathan: Get to know more people. The more people you know, the more people that know you and are willing to link to you.

Steph: What repels you the most from a blog (animations, in your face advertising, etc.)?

Jonathan: Obtrusive advertising including flash animated ads. They're distracting.

Steph: Do you make any direct money from your blog through advertising, product placements, etc.?

Jonathan: I make money through advertising including my own custom ad system, Text Link Ads, and hosting referral fees.

Steph: What is your best monetization method (Ads, affiliate marketing, etc.)?

Jonathan: It's actually a good blend that I've got right now between my custom ads, text link ads, and referral fees.

Steph: Do you find you get more from direct monetization of your blog or from opportunities that come because of the existence of your blog?

Jonathan: Oh, definitely from work opportunities. I'd love for ad revenue to hit a point where I don't have to work so hard but I'm not quite there yet.

Steph: What's your most interesting story related to your blog and blogging experience?

Jonathan: Nothing specifically stands out but I love going to conferences and having people come up and tell me that they enjoy my site. That's one of the best rewards of running it.

Steph: What's the one biggest opportunity that came to you because of your blog?

Jonathan: I got invited to Microsoft for a day which included meeting Bill Gates. That would never have happened had I not been running a blog.

Steph: Any other comments or thoughts you'd like to share?

Jonathan: Thank you for allowing me to take part in this.

Chapter 28

Manolo Blahnik

Manolo's Shoe Blog

http://shoeblogs.com

Since first appearing in October 2004, Manolo the Shoeblogger's website, has become one of the best read fashion sites on the internet. Manolo himself has been praised by authorities as various as the Wall Street Journal, Vogue, Fortune, the Sydney Morning Herald, and the Guardian.

Manolo has built a network of nine successful fashion and lifestyle blogs, employing a dozen bloggers. He's now in the process of starting up a sister network of Spanish-language fashion and lifestyle blogs. He also writes a weekly shoe advice column for the Washington Post Express, and has published a short comic work of philosophy entitled The Consolation of the Shoes.

Steph: What makes a blog successful according to you? Is it traffic, reach, revenue, etc.?

Manolo: The standard of blogging success is simple, do people read this blog everyday? If the answer is yes, than the blog has succeeded, even if the daily readers are only the tiny handful.

Too many peoples focus on building the giant mega-blog that crushes all in its path, using complete market dominance as the standard of success. What of the blogger who brings daily joy to two or three devoted readers, has this person not also succeeded?

Steph: When did you decide you finally reached success with your blog?

Manolo: The Manolo' s goals for his shoe blog were so low, that he thought he had succeeded as soon as he put up the first post. There were no other blogs devoted to the shoes, and so the Manolo achieved immediate success. Huzzah! Three cheers for the democratization of publishing!

Steph: How long does it take to become a successful blogger?

Manolo: Two days. On the first day the first visitor appears. On the second day this visitor comes back to see what's new. Success!

If he comes back the next, and the next day after than, and if the second person returns with him, well that is all gravy.

Steph: Who do you think are the most successful bloggers on the internet today?

Manolo: Ayyy! There are millions and millions of them! Too many to name.

Steph: Which five blogs do you regularly read?

Manolo:

The Bag Snob (**http://www.bagsnob.com/**)

The Coveted (**http://thecoveted.blogspot.com/**)

Boing Boing (**http://www.boingboing.net/**)

Ayyyy! (**http://ayyyy.com/**)

Cute Overload (**http://www.cuteoverload.com/**).

Steph: Which websites would you recommend for any new bloggers starting to blog?

Manolo: The wonderful thing about blogging is that each individual is completely free to pursue his or her own desires. Literally, as the Manolo has proven, one can start the blog about any topic and find thousands of readers. And so the Manolo would tell the aspiring blogger to blog about that which he loves the most, trusting that those who care about his topic will eventually find him.

And so the Manolo would tell the would-be blogger to find websites and blogs which speak to him personally, because of the topic, or the voice, or the personality of the blogger. Everyone finds inspiration in different places, and so why limit oneself.

Steph: Which book(s) would you recommend for new bloggers (these can range from marketing books, blogging books, etc.)?

Manolo: The Elements of Style by Strunk and White.

Steph: What is your most successful blog post ever?

Manolo: The post that has generated the most attention was when the Manolo called for the impeachment of President Bush because he wore the Crocs (**http://shoeblogs.com/2007/06/12/impeach-him/**). The Manolo is most decidedly anti-ugly shoe. It is the firmest of his political convictions.

Steph: What's your biggest tip on writing a successful blog post?

Manolo: Be funny. People love to laugh.

Steph: What's your best advice in regards to content and writing for bloggers?

Manolo: First learn to write the good, lively, entertaining prose, and then, second, do not be afraid of giving your readers the odd combination of the topics, or the peculiar view of the world, or the different way of approaching your subject. Do not be afraid to be seen as different, or even eccentric. Indeed, to be eccentric in the crowded world of the blogs is the strength.

Steph: How important do you think are the headlines of your blog articles?

Manolo: Moderately important. They are one more chance to make the small joke.

Steph: Do you spend any money and time on marketing?

Manolo: Yes, the Manolo has spent both time and money on marketing his new blogs. He has advertised, he has run contests, he has written letters asking for links. All of these help.

Steph: What are your main methods of marketing your blog?

Manolo: Sending polite emails to other bloggers suggesting that something the Manolo or one of his bloggers has written.

Steph: Which marketing tactic has surprised you the most in terms of its effectiveness?

Manolo: When the Manolo started his celebrity fashion gossip blog, Ayyyy!, the Manolo was surprised to find that Blogads helped spread word very well. And there was the side benefit that the blogs on which the Manolo advertised usually added to their blogrolls, without asking, the new blog that was being advertised!

Steph: What are your quick and short five best tips for blogging?

Manolo:

Be unique.

Be funny.

Be nice to other people.

Be generous with your links.

Be Happy.

Steph: What is the most common pitfall new bloggers generally fall into?

Manolo: Attempting to do too much, too fast. So many new bloggers burn out in the first months.

Steph: What repels you the most from a blog (animations, in your face advertising, etc.)?

Manolo: There are so many blogs that blog about exactly the same things in exactly the same way. Boring! The Manolo does not like to be bored, and so he moves on from boring blogs, never to return.

Steph: Do you make any direct money from your blog through advertising, product placements, etc.?

Manolo: Yes.

Steph: What is your best monetization method (Ads, affiliate marketing, etc.)?

Manolo: Ads and affiliate sales.

Steph: Do you find you get more from direct monetization of your blog or from opportunities that come because of the existence of your blog?

Manolo: Currently, the Manolo makes more from the direct monetization of his blog network than from the indirect methods.

Steph: What's your most interesting story related to your blog and blogging experience?

Manolo: For the humble shoeblogger, the most exciting moment was when the Maestro Manolo Blahnik the shoe designer, told the Times of London newspaper that he thought the Manolo's Shoe Blog was "hilarous". Ayyy! This was the Manolo the Shoeblogger proudest moment.

Steph: What's the one biggest opportunity that came to you because of your blog?

Manolo: There have been so many, the weekly shoe advice column in the Washington Post Express, the publication of the Manolo's short philosophical work, The Consolation of the Shoes, the opportunity to communicate with so many super fantastic peoples.

Steph: Thank you Manolo for the interview.

Chapter 29

Neil Patel

Quick Sprout

http://www.QuickSprout.com

Neil is not only a successful blogger, he's also a very successful businessman. He's the co-founder and CTO of Advantage Consulting Services. His company works with 22 of the Top 100 Technorati blogs and had revenues in the millions of dollars last year.

Neil is also the co-founder of Crazy Egg which offers one of the best visual visitor tracking tools on the Net.

What really sets Neil apart is that he's only 21 years old and still in school! However, according to Neil himself, "There isn't much to me, other than just running an Internet marketing firm, going to school, and writing a book. I am an Average Joe that eats Taco Bell a few times a week and loves movies and television". He's obviously modest too.

Steph: What makes a blog successful according to you? Is it traffic, reach, revenue, etc.?

Neil: Each person has a different view point on what makes a blog successful because each person's goals are different. My personal goal for my blog is to educate people and help them succeed in life. Due to this I measure my success based on traffic and RSS subscribership.

Steph: When did you decide you finally reached success with your blog?

Neil: I personally think I haven't reached success with my blog yet. I recently started a new blog called Quick Sprout and that is the main blog that I am blogging on now. The blog still has not reached 3000 RSS subscribers and I don't think I will be happy until the blog hits 100,000 subscribers.

Steph: How long does it take to become a successful blogger?

Neil: It truly depends on ones definition of success. If your goal is to educate or gain lots of traction I don't think a blog will be successful until after a year if not longer. Now granted you can grow very fast within 1 year of starting a blog, but because there are billions of people out in this world, I think it will take years before you truly gain a large readership.

Steph: Who do you think are the most successful bloggers on the internet today?

Neil: There are tons of successful blogs on the web and I wish I could name them all, but that would be too long of a list. Either way a few of them are Guy Kawasaki (**http://blog.guykawasaki.com/**), Copyblogger (**http://www.copyblogger.com/**), Shoemoney (**http://www.shoemoney.com/**), and Problogger (**http://www.problogger.net/**). All of these blogs educate readers for free, which is why I love reading them.

Steph: Which five blogs do you regularly read?

Neil:

TechCrunch (**http://www.techcrunch.com/**)

Mashable (**http://mashable.com/**)

Gigaom (**http://gigaom.com/**)

MicroPersuasion (**http://www.micropersuasion.com/**)

BoingBoing (**http://www.boingboing.net/**)

Steph: Which websites would you recommend for any new bloggers starting to blog?

Neil: Problogger (**http://www.problogger.net/**), Copyblogger (**http://www.copyblogger.com/**), Daily Blog Tips (**http://www.dailyblogtips.com/**), and JohnChow (**http://www.JohnChow.com/**) are just a few of the ones I would recommend to any new blogger. I realize many people may think John Chow is dumb, but if you ever get to know him you will realize he is a humble and wise guy who really enjoys helping new bloggers succeed.

Steph: Which book(s) would you recommend for new bloggers (these can range from marketing books, blogging books, etc.)?

Neil: There are probably hundreds of great books that bloggers can read, but sadly I don't read too many books. I prefer reading online content, such as blogs.

One book that new bloggers can benefit from is Naked Conversations, but the best way to learn in my opinion is by blogging. Think about the top bloggers out there, I highly doubt most of them read a book on blogging when they started, but instead learned by blogging on a regular basis.

Steph: What is your most successful blog post ever?

Neil: I don't think I have ever had one single blog post that stands out compared to the others. I have had a few popular ones that did well on the social web, but my favorite posts are usually ones that provide the most value to readers.

Steph: What's your biggest tip on writing a successful blog post?

Neil: The best blog posts are usually the ones that are short and sweet. So when writing content make sure you remove the fluff and just get down to the meat of the content.

Steph: What's your best advice in regards to content and writing for bloggers?

Neil: If you are writing for bloggers make sure you cover the basics as well as advanced tips. There will be a good amount of people who will leave nasty comments when you write 101 content, but if you think about it there are more blogging newbies than pros.

Steph: How important do you think are the headlines of your blog articles?

Neil: Headlines are the key in grabbing someone's attention. Think of readers as window shoppers and that they are only going to read your blog if they see something they like such as catchy headlines. Due to this I recommend reading blogs like Copyblogger and would even go as far as saying borrow some of their headlines. (I am pretty sure the Copyblogger team doesn't mind?)

Steph: Do you spend any money and time on marketing?

Neil: I spend a good amount of time marketing my blog. The way I market my blog is by writing content that others can benefit from. By doing this, readers naturally link to it as well as submit my blog to social sites like Digg which drives great traffic.

Steph: What are your main methods of marketing your blog?

Neil: Writing good content is my main way of marketing a blog. Other than that I would make sure a blog is search engine friendly and that you build relationships with other bloggers. By building relationships you will see more bloggers linking to you.

Steph: Which marketing tactic has surprised you the most in terms of its effectiveness?

Neil: Leveraging StumbleUpon is one method that has surprised me. I knew that it could drive traffic, but I never realized how many Stumblers actually convert into RSS subscribers.

Steph: What are your quick and short five best tips for blogging?

Neil:

Write good content

Write unique content

Always think about the reader/visitor first.

Optimize your blog for search engines.

Leverage the social web (digg, reddit, stumbleupon, ...)

Steph: What is the most common pitfall new bloggers generally fall into?

Neil: In many cases bloggers get discouraged when they don't see many comments or high traffic levels, so they stop blogging. The thing with blogging is that you have to be patient and it could take well over a year before you see decent traction to your blog.

Steph: If you knew what you know now when you first started, what's the one biggest tip you'd give yourself today?

Neil: Don't concentrate on the social web too much. If had built more relationships with other bloggers instead, my blog would have been much more popular due to cross promotion.

Steph: What repels you the most from a blog (animations, in your face advertising, etc.)?

Neil: Ads is the number one thing that irritates me. I don't care if you place 100 ads on you blog, but I care if you place too many ads within your content because it creates a bad user experience.

Steph: Do you make any direct money from your blog through advertising, product placements, etc.?

Neil: I do have ads on Pronet Advertising, so I make a bit of money. As for Quick Sprout there are no ads on it currently and hopefully it will stay that way.

Steph: What is your best monetization method (Ads, affiliate marketing, etc.)?

Neil: It is going to vary for each blog. The only way you can figure out the best way to monetize a blog is to do a lot of testing because what works on one blog may not work on the next.

Steph: Do you find you get more from direct monetization of your blog or from opportunities that come because of the existence of your blog?

Neil: I get more from opportunities that come because of the existence of my blog. Most of my opportunities are consulting related.

Steph: What's your most interesting story related to your blog and blogging experience?

Neil: The most interesting story related to my blogging experience is not one that I have written. Instead it is how I have helped 22 of the Technorati top 100 to become more popular. I have done this through SEO, giving advice on content writing, as well as helping them leverage the social web.

Steph: What's the one biggest opportunity that came to you because of your blog?

Neil: To me my biggest opportunity has been speaking engagements. In most cases these speaking engagements lose me money, but I love them because I get to educate others as well as tell them the truth. Most speakers tell people fluff and I am known for telling people how things actually are (or so I hope).

Steph: Any other comments or thoughts you'd like to share?

Neil: Keep on blogging and never give up. Sooner or later something valuable is going to come out of your blogging experience, but you just have to give it some time.

Chapter 30

Pamela Slim

Escape from Cubicle Nation

http://www.EscapeFromCubicleNation.com

Pamela Slim is a seasoned coach and writer who helps frustrated employees in corporate jobs break out and start their own business. A former corporate manager and entrepreneur herself for more than a decade, she deeply understands the questions and concerns faced by first-time entrepreneurs. Her expertise in personal and business change was developed through many years consulting inside corporations such as Cisco Systems, Hewlett-Packard and Charles Schwab, where she coached thousands of executives, managers and employees.

Pamela has trained with "the best-known life coach in America," New York Times bestseller and O Magazine columnist Martha Beck. She is married with three kids and lives in Mesa, Arizona.

Steph: What makes a blog successful according to you? Is it traffic, reach, revenue, etc.?

Pamela: A blog is successful when it provides content that is extremely useful or entertaining to its target readers. That metric is the "gift that keeps on giving" and feeds any other desired goals such as unique visitors per month, incoming links, advertising revenue or press attention.

Steph: When did you decide you finally reached success with your blog?

Pamela: Although getting hat-tips from high-profile bloggers like Guy Kawasaki, Tom Peters, Seth Godin and Kathy Sierra was enormously gratifying, the way I really knew I was hitting the mark were the hundreds of emails I got from my target audience. When people wrote saying that my blog helped them quit their day job to start a business, I knew I was doing something right.

Steph: How long does it take to become a successful blogger?

Pamela: It all depends on how you define success.

If you want to develop a devoted readership and consistent traffic, I think it takes at least a year of steady writing so that you have a wide variety of content for people to read. Given the millions of people blogging, if you are not a very talented writer and don't have a lot of valuable information to contribute to your target audience, chances are your blog won't have the outward trappings of success like lots of subscribers, high Technorati ranking or ad revenue. But if you do it for love, who cares about those other definition of success?

Steph: Who do you think are the most successful bloggers on the internet today?

Pamela: I am more familiar with business bloggers since that is my scope of interest. In this group I would put Seth Godin (**http://sethgodin.typepad.com/**), Guy Kawasaki (**http://blog.guykawasaki.com/**) and Darren Rowse (**http://www.problogger.com/**).

Steph: Which five blogs do you regularly read?

Pamela: The blogs I enjoy reading are:

Guy Kawasaki—How to Change the World (**http://blog.guykawasaki.com/**)

Kathy Sierra—Creating Passionate Users (**http://headrush.typepad.com/**)

Ramit Sethi—I Will Teach You to Be Rich (**http://www.iwillteachyoutoberich.com/**)

Garr Reynolds—Presentation Zen (**http://www.presentationzen.com/**)

Leo Babauta—Zen Habits (**http://zenhabits.net/**)

Steph: Which websites would you recommend for any new bloggers starting to blog?

Pamela: For those wanting to understand blogging for blogging's sake, I recommend Darren Rowse's ProBlogger (**http://www.problogger.net/**). Otherwise, search Technorati (**http://www.technorati.com/**) for both the most popular blogs on the internet and the most popular blogs in your field of expertise. Spend a few weeks reading and commenting on these blogs, and you will soon get a feel for what kind of content is useful and interesting to read.

Steph: Which book(s) would you recommend for new bloggers (these can range from marketing books, blogging books, etc.)?

Pamela: For people new to the whole concept of blogging: Blogwild by Andy Wibbels. For more technically oriented people: Clear Blogging by Bob Walsh. (disclaimer: I wrote the forward to this book)

Steph: What is your most successful blog post ever?

Pamela: My most successful post was "Open letter to CXOs across the corporate world." (**http://www.escapefromcubiclenation.com/get_a_life_blog/2006/05/open_letter_to_.html**) It was my heartfelt rant at corporate executives based on what I had experienced for the past ten years as a consultant in hundreds of corporations across the U.S. It hit a nerve with managers and employees alike, drew huge traffic, press attention and over 500 incoming links to my blog.

Steph: What's your biggest tip on writing a successful blog post?

Pamela: Write from your soul. It is very easy to get caught up in your ego and worry about what people will think of your ideas. This will stunt your writing. Write from the deepest part of yourself and you will discover an abundance of creativity. If you write a business blog, I also suggest including specific recommendations. People want to apply your ideas, so help them do so.

Steph: What's your best advice in regards to content and writing for bloggers?

Pamela: Create a clear picture of your readers and put yourself in their shoes. I use the following questions about my audience to guide the content for my blog:

What problems do they face?

What really scares them?

What is not being said on this subject on other news sources or blogs?

What can I share that will make their life easier?

How can I make them feel more supported and confident?

Who can I put them in contact with (via links or references) that will give them good information and advice?

What will be fun and interesting to write about?

Steph: How important do you think are the headlines of your blog articles?

Pamela: Headlines are extremely important in blogging. Many people subscribe to multiple feeds and scan huge lists of posts looking for something compelling enough to read at length. Google searches turn up thousands of one-line results. So choose headlines that will grab attention.

Steph: Do you spend any money and time on marketing?

Pamela: If you consider writing posts, reading other blogs and commenting on them "marketing," yes, I spend lots of time marketing my blog. But I don't use any paid methods, such as Google ads or specific campaigns.

Steph: What are your main methods of marketing your blog?

Pamela: I try to write consistently on topics that are of great interest to my readers. This is the best way to get lots of trackback posts, which is the key to blog promotion. I visit other blogs and comment. I also mention my blog in any press article, email signature or author biography.

Steph: Which marketing tactic has surprised you the most in terms of its effectiveness?

Pamela: The counterintuitive tactic of "don't actively market your blog, just write good stuff." People who are overzealous in link exchange or who hound "A-Listers" to write about them are usually written off as immature or desperate. Good old-fashioned relationship building is the best way to build an audience for your blog. Be responsive and kind to your commenter, and be interested and helpful to experts in your field.

Steph: What are your quick and short five best tips for blogging?

Pamela:

Write about the things that you can't stop thinking about.

Never forget who your audience is.

Make it easy for people to follow your advice.

Be yourself.

Be generous with links to others in your posts.

Steph: What is the most common pitfall new bloggers generally fall into?

Pamela: Many new bloggers get sucked into statistic paranoia. They spend so much time tracking how many visitors or subscribers they have that they forget to put their energies into writing quality posts. As soon as you start to select content just to provoke incoming links, you are doomed. Stay true to the purpose of your blog, and the audience that is meant to come will.

Steph: If you knew what you know now when you first started, what's the one biggest tip you'd give yourself today?

Pamela: It may sound strange, but I don't think I would change much about my blogging journey. I didn't even know what a blog was before I started, and that naiveté pushed me to learn as much as I could as I went along. Advice I would give others is don't think you have to be an expert in blogging before you start. Let the reader interaction guide you.

Steph: What repels you the most from a blog (animations, in your face advertising, etc.)?

Pamela: Three things repel me from a blog: screaming advertising, boring content and no blogger profile. I don't mind a bit of advertising if it fits in the overall design and flow of the blog. But Google ads right in the middle of the introductory paragraph send me running. Boring content for me means words with no opinion, and topics that don't educate, provoke or entertain. No blogger profile makes me think the person is either too lazy to say who they are or not confident enough to own their opinions. If they are writing anonymously out of self-protection, that is fine, as long as they say so. And I always like to see a picture.

Steph: Do you make any direct money from your blog through advertising, product placements, etc.?

Pamela: Up to now, I have chosen not to run advertising on my blog. I get a handful of change in Amazon affiliate commissions from the recommended books which run along my sidebar, but that is about it.

Steph: Do you find you get more from direct monetization of your blog or from opportunities that come because of the existence of your blog?

Pamela: I don't blog for money but I have gotten tons of work, writing opportunities and press coverage from it. All of my coaching clients come through my blog.

Steph: What's your most interesting story related to your blog and blogging experience?

Pamela: What's the one biggest opportunity that came to you because of your blog? It is hard to choose just one since it has been such a magical mystery tour, filled with amazing opportunities. So I will cheat and share two. 1) I was invited to meet and interview Gloria Steinem in New York as part of the launch of a women-owned radio station, and 2) I was asked to write a guest post for the New York Times.

Steph: Any other comments or thoughts you'd like to share?

Pamela: Thanks for the opportunity Stephane—I really appreciate being included! I look forward to reading the book.

Chapter

31

Patrick McKenzie

MicroISV on a Shoestring

http://microisvjournal.wordpress.com

Patrick McKenzie is the author of MicroISV on a Shoestring, a blog focused on running small software businesses (where ISV stands for Independent Software Vendor). Or to put it in Patrick's words "you know, one of us folks selling software over the Internet as we lounge around at home in our pyjamas."

Patrick started his blog to accompany the project that launched his entrepreneurial career, Bingo Card Creator (http://www.bingocardcreator.com/). He was an english teacher (among many other things) and really hated having to waste time prepping for classes when he could be helping students. One activity he loved, but which took an hour of his life every time he ran it, was vocabulary bingo. Patrick figured there had to be a better way to do this so he created a program and decided it might actually be worth something to other people too. He then opened a business to sell his software and his blog followed shortly afterwards to chronicle his experiences in more-or-less real time.

Steph: What makes a blog successful according to you? Is it traffic, reach, revenue, etc.?

Patrick: A blog is successful if it meets the blogger's goals for it. Nothing more, nothing less. I was inspired to get off my duff and actually open my business largely on the basis of one blog I was a regular reader of and one blog post I just happened across one day. My goal for my blog, when I was just a guy with a half-written bingo program and a dream, was that someday people would look at it and say "Wow, you know, I could open a business, too."

Steph: When did you decide you finally reached success with your blog?

Patrick: The first time I heard someone say "Thanks, you pushed me to start my own business" I knew I had succeeded, and I have collected an impressive number of similar successes along the way.

Steph: How long does it take to become a successful blogger?

Patrick: That depends entirely on what goals you set. If your goal is to replace your income blogging, which I have a sneaking suspicion it might be if you are reading this book, the answer is most probably "more time than you will remain dedicated to this project". I suggest starting with modest, achievable goals and gradually working your way up. (The same technique works well for small businesses, too. And make no mistake, once you have a blog, you have a small business, whether you realize it or not.)

Speaking of timescales in blogging—recognize that you will be blogging until you stop blogging. That sounds simple, but many people start out with a burst of post-every-day fever, which they cannot sustain over the long haul. Pick a pace which is predictable and sustainable.

Steph: Who do you think are the most successful bloggers on the internet today?

Patrick: The wonderful thing about defining success as achievement of your goals is that it makes it possible for everyone to succeed simultaneously, without having to say X is more successful than Y is more successful than Z.

Steph: Which five blogs do you regularly read?

Patrick: I read at least a dozen. My favourites of the moment are SEOMoz (search engine optimization), SEO Book (more search engine optimization—check out Aaron Wall's article in this book, incidentally), Instapundit (news & commentary), Successful Software (software marketing), and Zen of Design (commentary on game design). What can I say, I have eclectic tastes.

Steph: Which websites would you recommend for any new bloggers starting to blog?

Patrick: Google can help you find writing and HTML resources better than I can. I recommend, instead, that you get familiar with two groups of websites in your niche: the folks who have achieved something close to what you want to achieve, and the folks who are on the path to that success but just a wee bit farther than you are. The first give you examples to emulate and objectives to strive for, and the second should become your new best friends, because a) they're not too busy yet that they have millions of admirers and b) their support can really kick start your blog and help you both get closer to your goals.

Steph: Which book(s) would you recommend for new bloggers (these can range from marketing books, blogging books, etc.)?

Patrick: This might be heretical for an ex-English teacher, but I think the best information specific to blogging is not written on paper. You can certainly apply humanity's accumulated store of printed knowledge to blogging, though. I recommend reading both Blink and The Long Tail, with an eye on how you can use the high-level concepts they discuss to perform effective low-level Internet marketing.

Steph: What is your most successful blog post ever?

Patrick: Given that I am intrinsically motivated, that is a difficult question to answer. I have several longer posts about the theory and practice of online marketing, and I consider these my best work. My personal favourite is "Ranking For An Arbitrary Search Engine Query" (**http://microisvjournal.wordpress.com/2007/05/30/ranking-for-an-arbitrary-organic-search-query/**), where I introduced the concept of "snowflake queries". You see, half of all search engine queries are like snowflakes—they are individually unique but if you view them from a higher level of abstraction you can generalize over them. For example, if you ask 100 teachers to say "Type something into Google to find a bingo card activity for class on Friday", roughly 20 of them will type "bingo cards", but roughly 60 of them will type sixty different variations of "bingo card activity", "bingo cards for teachers", "need bingo cards for my class", "How do I do a lesson with bingo?", etc etc. If you can learn how to harness snowflake queries, any business you run on the Internet, including your blog, will benefit substantially.

Numerically, my most successful post is "Free Bingo Cards" (**http://microisvjournal.wordpress.com/2007/03/16/free-bingo-cards/**), which contains exactly what it says: free bingo cards, on a rotating selection of themes. Thousands of people visit it every month—probably a quarter of the total traffic to all the sites I control. Content, as they say, is king. (Incidentally, that post wouldn't have been nearly as successful had my peer group not spontaneously decided to help me out by linking to it. Having friends is a wonderful thing.)

Steph: What's your biggest tip on writing a successful blog post?

Patrick: A blog post is a product. It fills a need in the market, it has competitors, and the prospective customers for the product have virtually infinite choices among other products. Make sure that your blog post provides something of value which they can't get anywhere else, and they will have no choice but to fill that need from you.

Steph: What's your best advice in regards to content and writing for bloggers?

Patrick: There are two types of reading behaviour on the Internet: scanning and reading. If your content is not scannable, it will be skipped by almost all scanning readers (remember, infinite competitors are just one click away!) That is the bad news. The worse news is that almost every Internet user is scanning for the majority of their online experience, so you essentially have to make your site cater to the behaviour at least part of the time.

I personally can't stand the "Top Ten Ways To Write A Blog Post" type articles, as aside from being boring and aesthetically unpleasant they turn your blog into a commodity provider of lists. Instead, absorb the lessons that style of writing provides while continuing to have unique positioning for your blog. The important lessons are "titles which promise immediate benefit are a good idea" and "judicious use of formatting such as bullet points, bold text, and pictures can turn a scanning surfer into an engaged, active reader."

Steph: How important do you think are the headlines of your blog articles?

Patrick: They are critical for getting your post noticed before gatekeepers, such as other bloggers and the social networking sites, have determined that the content of that post is significantly better than the background noise of the Internet. After a blog post is noticed, the title doesn't matter nearly as much, because people will be going to read it not because of what the title promises but because of what the recommendation from an authority promises. For example, if a blogger who I have been reading for years says "Hey, I just saw this excellent post about Internet marketing", I will read it, without necessarily even being told of the gist of the article let alone the title.

A good title can also help you in getting organic search traffic for years after the post is up. Many people (and even more automated systems, like social network sites and blog aggregators) will link to a post by its title. That, plus the title appearing prominently on the page and in strategic locations in the code, will cause the post to generally rank fairly well for its title relative to other phrases it contains which are similarly competitive. For example, "free bingo cards" is a fairly competitive search result in my field, and my post would likely not rank nearly as well for that if the title had been "Here is a freebie for you" instead of "Free Bingo Cards".

Accordingly, you generally will want your titles to be descriptive, attractive, and filled with promise of value to the reader, rather than having them be in-jokes, clever wordplay, and the like. However, after you have reached a certain level of traffic, and for posts which reach a certain level of authority in the field, the title drops from "paramount importance" to merely being "important". For example, if I were to put up another valuable article about customer service tomorrow (one of the things my readers largely trust me to be a reliably insightful on), I can be fairly confident that post would start a conversation even with a less than optimal title.

Steph: Do you spend any money and time on marketing?

Patrick: I spend a good deal of time and money marketing for my business. As for my blog? No, not really. I write about what I want to write about, and as folks find that valuable they generally find me rather than me finding them. However, since part of my beat as a small business owner is marketing, I'll tell you what tips you can use for marketing on the Internet anyhow.

Steph: What are your main methods of marketing your blog?

Patrick: I mentioned earlier that you should identify a group of peers who are just slightly above you on the hypothetical totem pole. You want to be incestuously close to these people—put them in your feedreader, comment on their posts when you have something valuable to say, and link to them regularly. Attention is the currency of the blogosphere, and he who pays it to people who are not already swimming in it will receive it in return.

Steph: Which marketing tactic has surprised you the most in terms of its effectiveness?

Patrick: While I generally stress the importance of marketing a blog among its relative peers, there is something to be said for a cheerful disregard for the word "impossible". I would have thought emailing several dozen extraordinarily successful blog authors (and one guy living in a ricefield in central Japan) with a proposal to write a book would have resulted in nothing but spam complaints. You're reading the book now, so that shows what I know.

Similarly, my most visible post (other than Free Bingo Cards) resulted from me going onto the blog of someone who is extraordinarily influential in my niche, saying "I respectfully but strongly disagree with your approach here. I wrote up the reasons for it on my blog, here is the link", and having many people say the plucky nobody was (that one, single time) more right than the authority. That post got widely picked up throughout my niche, including by probably the most influential blogger in it, and has been viewed a few tens of thousand times. (Which is a decent day's work for some bloggers, but greatly exceeds my usual reach.)

Steph: What are your quick and short five best tips for blogging?

Patrick:

Snappy, Factual, Value-laden Titles

Judicious Use of Bold Subject Headings

A Unique, Consistent, Personal Voice

Link to your peers

Maintain a comfortable pace

Steph: What is the most common pitfall new bloggers generally fall into?

Patrick: Writing about yourself. The reader doesn't want to hear about you, unless you are interesting to him already, and that process takes time (rather like dating, actually). They want to hear about themselves—about things which matter to them and information they can use. Write about your readers and you will never lack for them.

Steph: If you knew what you know now when you first started, what's the one biggest tip you'd give yourself today?

Patrick: Host the blog yourself, rather than putting it at yourblog.wordpress.com or a similar provider. There are a variety of reasons for this, but trust me, you will be much, much happier with yourself later if you have 100% control than if you sacrifice it for ease of use for your first week or two. This isn't a technically involved process—most web hosts can have you up and running with a new blog on a new domain in about 5-15 minutes, and you can learn as you go.

Steph: What repels you the most from a blog (animations, in your face advertising, etc.)?

Patrick: "Top Ten Reasons I Could Care Less About This Blog Post". That screams to me that the post will be formulaic, cursory, and commodity information—the exact opposite of what I want to spend my limited time reading.

Steph: Do you make any direct money from your blog through advertising, product placements, etc.?

Patrick: My blog is primarily about my business, and theorizing about similar businesses, rather than about my customers for my business. Accordingly, it drives rather few direct sales for me. Call it about $100 worth a month. I have steadfastly refused to monetize with product placement or advertising because I believe to do so would compromise my value to my readers.

Steph: What is your best monetization method (Ads, affiliate marketing, etc.)?

Patrick: As noted, I don't directly monetize my blog. In terms of what part of it makes the most money, the fact that I am a fairly well-known blogger in my wee little niche probably attracts more links (and thus organic searchers) to my product's website than I would have without the blog, and more organic searchers translates directly into more sales.

Steph: Do you find you get more from direct monetization of your blog or from opportunities that come because of the existence of your blog?

Patrick: I have had some interesting opportunities develop as a result of my blog. One is writing this book. Another was being approached by a Product Manager at Google to develop a case study for their Conversion Optimizer, which is a cost-per-click marketing product which I was an early adopter of. Since my blog is radically transparent about the cost, revenue, and traffic figures for my business, I was literally the only place to go on the Internet to hear substantiated claims about how Conversion Optimizer worked out for real people. As a result, I got just a few more links than the next guy covering the topic and, whammo, there I am on Google ranking as a top authority on their product. That, plus the fact that I said (truthfully) that it worked out extraordinarily well for me, drew the attention of the world's biggest online authority to my little section of cyberspace. The cooperation will draw an amount of exposure to my business which is gigantic relative to its size, and additionally "Partnered with Google to ..." makes a nice bullet point on the resume. Plus, they sent me a laptop bag with the Google logo on it. The geek bling makes me the envy of my programmer friends.

Steph: What's your most interesting story related to your blog and blogging experience?

Patrick: When I was just starting blogging, a single link or word of praise, from anybody, made me feel like the fan singled out by a rockstar at a concert. Then, one day one of my readers (Rizal Al-Mashoor—**http://www.rizalalmashoor.com/blog/**) sent me an email. He had spent a considerable chunk of his own time making a widget that would let you read my blog in chronological order (**http://www.rizalalmashoor.com/reader/microisvjournal/**), so that he could share it with his buddies who weren't there when it started but could benefit from the progression my business went through. I was amazingly humbled that someone would find what I had written that worthwhile, and sent him a thank-you note and promptly linked to the utility from my blog. Rizal was enormously flattered. Then it dawned on me: for at least one person, I was now the rockstar. That is the beauty of the Internet: in a world with virtually infinite niches, we can all be rockstars in our own little ways. I can almost guarantee you that is or will be somebody out there for whom Rizal is the rockstar. (Also, going back to my point about peers: since I'm just a wee bit more influential than somebody just starting out in my niche, pitching a project like that to be is almost guaranteed to draw my immediate attention. Thus, if you (like Rizal) are trying to get in on the ground floor, the most reliably valuable people to try influencing are the ones who are just a wee bit better known, more influential, etc, than you are.)

Steph: What's the one biggest opportunity that came to you because of your blog?

Patrick: See the Google bit from the previous question.

Steph: Any other comments or thoughts you'd like to share?

Patrick: For whatever your definition of success is, it will be easier writing about something you love than about something which you merely believe is advantageous. Passion is something which comes across clearly in writing—it infuses mere words with the author's unique voice, and that gets you half of the way to being heard over the endless sea of garbage that is the Internet. The other half of the equation is making sure your unique voice is saying something of valuable to your community of readers. If you are passionate about what they are passionate about, if you are passionate about them, then you have this blogging thing essentially in the bag. If not, all the keyword optimization, link building strategies, and well-written titles in the world will not save you.

Chapter 32

Penelope Trunk

Brazen Careerist

http://blog.penelopetrunk.com

Penelope writes career advice for a new generation of workers. She explains why much of the old advice is outdated and irrelevant in today's workplace. She's especially known for test-driving her advice before giving it. Her own career choices have been featured by Time magazine and the Guardian as examples of the new issues people face at work today. Both the New York Times and Business Week cited her writing as especially in tune with today's new workplace.

Penelope has spent ten years as a marketing executive in the software industry. She then founded two companies of her own. She's endured an IPO, a merger, and a bankruptcy. Prior to working in the executive world, Penelope was a professional beach volleyball player.

Today, Penelope is a columnist at Boston Globe, and her syndicated column runs in more than 200 publications worldwide. She has written the book Brazen Careerist: The New Rules for Success. She is also the author of the famous blog Brazen Careerist.

Steph: What makes a blog successful according to you? Is it traffic, reach, revenue, etc.?

Penelope: It helps you reach your goals—either career or personal.

Steph: When did you decide you finally reached success with your blog?

Penelope: I love blogging, and I am able to support my family doing it. So on some level, success is being able to support my family doing something I love. On another level, I am redefining success constantly, because once I reach a goal, I set a higher goal.

Steph: How long does it take to become a successful blogger?

Penelope: I'm sure it's different for each person. Each person has different goals, different definitions of success.

Steph: Who do you think are the most successful bloggers on the internet today?

Penelope: The people who are using their blog to reach their goals.

Steph: Which five blogs do you regularly read?

Penelope:

Guy Kawasaki's (**http://blog.guykawasaki.com/**)

Lifehacker (**http://lifehacker.com/**)

Get Rich Slowly (**http://getrichslowly.org/blog/**)

Employee Evolution (**http://www.employeeevolution.com/**)

TechCrunch (**http://www.techcrunch.com/**)

Steph: Which websites would you recommend for any new bloggers starting to blog?

Penelope: ProBlogger (**http://www.Problogger.com**)

Steph: Which book(s) would you recommend for new bloggers (these can range from marketing books, blogging books, etc.)?

Penelope: The Sensual Woman. I read it when I was a kid and I was trying to figure out what sex was. I didn't really understand—at that point—why people would even want to have sex. But what I did understand was that if you were your real self, and just did what felt right, you would meet the definition of "good in bed." And then, very quickly, I realized that this book applied to everything in life—just be your true self and people will see that you enjoy yourself and they will see the true you and whoever you are, seeing that will be interesting. I think a lot of bloggers are scared to be their true selves on their blog, but so much of blogging is about the blogger's personality. So people should read this book—to understand how fundamental it is to just be yourself.

Steph: What is your most successful blog post ever?

Penelope: The one about my first day of marriage counseling (**http://blog.penelopetrunk.com/2007/07/05/my-first-day-of-marriage-counseling/**)

Steph: What's your biggest tip on writing a successful blog post?

Penelope: Find a very popular topic and then write at the very edge of that topic. If you write in the center, that's where everyone else is and it will be hard to present something that is unique. If you write at the edge, and throw in stuff not totally related to your topic area, then both you and your readers will find surprises in that intersection of the new stuff and your topic.

Steph: What's your best advice in regards to content and writing for bloggers?

Penelope: Keep writing.

Steph: How important do you think are the headlines of your blog articles?

Penelope: Very important. It's how people decide if they will read or not.

Steph: Do you spend any money and time on marketing?

Penelope: No.

Steph: What are your main methods of marketing your blog?

Penelope: Write good posts. Join the online conversation that is bigger than my own blog.

Steph: Which marketing tactic has surprised you the most in terms of its effectiveness?

Penelope: Being nice. A blog is a conversation, not a soapbox. So when I engage my readers, and when I talk with other bloggers, via their blogs, people really respond in a positive way.

Steph: Do you make any direct money from your blog through advertising, product placements, etc.?

Penelope: Yes. I earn a six-figure income from my blog.

Steph: What is your best monetization method (Ads, affiliate marketing, etc.)?

Penelope: I sell my blog posts to print and online publishers.

Steph: Do you find you get more from direct monetization of your blog or from opportunities that come because of the existence of your blog?

Penelope: I think that long-term, the blog opens a lot of doors that are new career opportunities more than direct dollar income.

Steph: What's your most interesting story related to your blog and blogging experience?

Penelope: I try harder in marriage counseling because so many people are reading about my counseling experience on my blog.

Steph: What's the one biggest opportunity that came to you because of your blog?

Penelope: I sold equity in my blog and spun off a separate company.

Steph: Any other comments or thoughts you'd like to share?

Penelope: I don't think people should look at blogging as a money making venture. Very few people can make money off of a blog. But blogging opens tons of doors—via networking, especially, because bloggers have access to people they would not otherwise get access to. Blogging is a great way to build a career if you know what you want from your career. This doesn't necessarily mean that blogging itself is a great career. It's probably best as a means to create stability in one's career by getting to the top of one's field. I think bloggers in general are smart, dedicated and exceptionally well-informed. Blogging takes a ton of time, so most people are blogging about career related stuff because that's the only arena that is worth the time commitment. So it makes sense that bloggers would be great hires, and blogging, therefore, will help people get to the top of their field.

Chapter 33

Ramit Sethi

I Will Teach You To Be Rich

http://www.iwillteachyoutoberich.com/

Ramit Sethi is the founder and author of the blog "I Will Teach You To Be Rich" which is about personal finance and entrepreneurship. It hosts over 150,000 readers per month and has been featured in the Wall Street Journal, New York Times, and Yahoo Finance.

Ramit is also the co-founder and VP of marketing for PBwiki, a venture-backed online startup that hosts millions of users per month and recently raised $2m in venture-capital funding. PBwiki hosts hundreds of thousands of educational and business wikis.

He is the co-author of Recruit or Die: How Any Business Can Beat the Big Guys in the War for Young Talent, which advises companies how to recruit top college graduates. His second book, I Will Teach You To Be Rich, will be available shortly.

Ramit graduated from Stanford in 2005 with undergraduate and graduate degrees in technology, psychology, and sociology, and he currently lives in San Francisco.

Steph: What makes a blog successful according to you? Is it traffic, reach, revenue, etc.?

Ramit: Stats are overemphasized with blogs. I think a blog is successful when your message resonates with your readers and you have real behavioral change from what you're writing about. For example, one of my friends writes a blog with a very small readership—but a very influential one. Despite having few readers, he recently got an email from one of the most successful entrepreneurs in Silicon Valley inviting him out to lunch. His blog is successful.

Steph: When did you decide you finally reached success with your blog?

Ramit: When someone came up to me at a bar and asked me if I was Ramit from iwillteachyoutoberich, that was a big turning point. My friends thought I paid the guy to come up and say that.

Also, when I surveyed my readers asking them how my blog had changed their attitudes or behaviors about money, I got back hundreds of responses from people who had set up Roth IRAs, helped their parents with their finances, or just started managing their money properly. That was probably my favorite post ever.

Steph: How long does it take to become a successful blogger?

Ramit: There are no magic answers! It took me about six months to have anyone reading my stuff, and that was by writing good content and telling people about it. Other bloggers had more traffic within 2 months, if that's how you define success. It just depends on your definition of success. To dig into that, I'd try to understand who you're writing for—is it yourself or your audience? If it's your audience, I think you're successful when you write posts that resonate and make people think, debate, and change.

Steph: Who do you think are the most successful bloggers on the internet today?

Ramit:

Seth Godin (http://sethgodin.typepad.com/)

J.D. of Get Rich Slowly (http://www.getrichslowly.org/blog/)

Ben Casnocha (http://ben.casnocha.com/)

Michael Arrington (http://www.techcrunch.com/)

Penelope Trunk (http://blog.penelopetrunk.com/)

Kimber from Client K (http://www.clientk.com/)

Tim Ferriss (http://fourhourworkweek.com/blog/)

Steph: Which five blogs do you regularly read?

Ramit: All of the above

Steph: Which websites would you recommend for any new bloggers starting to blog?

Ramit: I'd recommend reading some of the top blogs on http://www.bloglines.com/topblogs for about 30 minutes. Then start writing! Nothing is more important than writing good stuff.

Steph: Which book(s) would you recommend for new bloggers (these can range from marketing books, blogging books, etc.)?

Ramit: Seth Godin's books are all great, especially Purple Cow. My blogger friends tend to have lots of stuff going on, so I'd also recommend Getting Things Done. But most importantly, I'd recommend reading the best books on the topic you're writing about. You just can't compare a blog post with the depth of research needed to write a good book.

Steph: What is your most successful blog post ever?

Ramit: One of my most popular was "The $28,000 Question: Why Are We All Hypocrites About Weddings?" (**http://www.iwillteachyoutoberich.com/blog/the-28000-question-why-are-we-all-hypocrites-about-weddings**). I wrote about how we all insist we want a simple wedding, but when it comes around, we almost always get an expensive wedding. Since the average wedding is (debatably) $28,000, isn't it funny how we all think we'll be different? Instead of insisting that we'll have a simple wedding, I urged people to get real and start saving for the average wedding cost. If they looked at the numbers, they'd realize that they needed to be saving hundreds of dollars per month. The post got a lot of attention because we almost all get married, and looking at the real numbers was sobering.

Steph: What's your biggest tip on writing a successful blog post?

Ramit: Opinions are cheap. Try to get some data to back up your posts. Barring that, examples are good.

Steph: What's your best advice in regards to content and writing for bloggers?

Ramit: Focus on the content, not stats! When most of my blogger friends started out, they spent more time checking stats than they did writing. That's crazy! Good content comes first, then readers.

Steph: How important do you think are the headlines of your blog articles?

Ramit: Extraordinarily important. The difference between "Conscious Spending: How My Friend Spends $21,000/year Going Out" and "Know What You Spend" is vast.

Steph: Do you spend any money and time on marketing?

Ramit: When I started, I spent about 5 hours per week reading other bloggers who I admired and reaching out to them. These days, I spend most of my time writing.

Steph: What are your main methods of marketing your blog?

Ramit: I reach out to other bloggers and respond to journalists, but the most effective marketing I can do is to write a really good post.

Steph: Which marketing tactic has surprised you the most in terms of its effectiveness?

Ramit: Spending 15-20 hours on a detailed post and watching lots of people come. In terms of the thing that had very little effectiveness on marketing, changing the design of your blog is mostly about ego, not making your blog more successful.

Steph: What are your quick and short five best tips for blogging?

Ramit:

Focus on the content! Write posts that add something new to the conversation.

Go one step further than others and use original data or interviews.

Barring that, using photos (especially of babies) is a well-known trick that, sadly, works.

Make sure you tell the right people about it. For example, if you write, say, a post on how much weddings will cost, you should probably tell all the wedding bloggers about it.

Helping other people is a great way to get your feet wet blogging. Write a guest post for a popular blogger. Or offer to do free research for them. Keith Ferrazzi's book covers this really well.

Steph: What is the most common pitfall new bloggers generally fall into?

Ramit: New bloggers check their stats too much and try to make money too fast! Once you're writing great stuff and people enjoy your blog as a daily (or weekly) regular feature, you'll have lots of options for how to optimize your design, stats, and money. First, focus on the content. I've written a post on this called "I Hate Bloggers Who Waste Their Time On Stats." (**http://www.iwillteachyoutoberich.com/blog/i-hate-bloggers-who-waste-their-time-on-stats**)

Steph: If you knew what you know now when you first started, what's the one biggest tip you'd give yourself today?

Ramit: Writing is really hard to scale, so try to figure out how to make a community out of your readers. It's easier said than done.

Steph: What repels you the most from a blog (animations, in your face advertising, etc.)?

Ramit: Boring content.

Steph: Do you make any direct money from your blog through advertising, product placements, etc.?

Ramit: For the past three years, I haven't directly monetized my blog (except for a small ebook I wrote). In September 2007, I started a 3-month experiment to see how blog advertising would work out.

Steph: What is your best monetization method (Ads, affiliate marketing, etc.)?

Ramit: Affiliate ads seem to be working pretty well for products that I recommend, like ING accounts.

Steph: Do you find you get more from direct monetization of your blog or from opportunities that come because of the existence of your blog?

Ramit: This is a pet peeve of mine: when bloggers try to make money from their blog before creating something useful. In my case, I make far more from indirect opportunities like speaking and book deals than from direct ads. (I've written more about this in a post called "On Greed and Speed."—http://www.iwillteachyoutoberich.com/blog/on-greed-and-speed)

Steph: What's the one biggest opportunity that came to you because of your blog?

Ramit: A book deal for the I Will Teach You To Be Rich book, which will be published in late 2008. Also, I was able to surprise my parents with an article in my hometown paper, in which I thanked them for inspiring me to write. My mom told me, "I've never seen my name in print!" And that made it all worth it.

Steph: Thank you Ramit for the interview.

Chapter

34

Rob Walling

Software By Rob

http://www.softwarebyrob.com

Rob is the author of the popular software blog Software by Rob where he discusses hiring, managing, motivating, and retaining software developers, with a focus on software startups.

Rob owns a software consulting firm called The Numa Group that performs ASP.NET development for clients throughout the United States. He also sells DotNetInvoice, the only ASP.NET Invoicing System on the market. It's a powerful web application that allows you to invoice clients and collect real time payments on your website, along with many other great features for small businesses.

Rob has worked as a consultant, a freelance developer, the development manager for the City of Pasadena, and a team lead for the world's largest prepaid credit card company. Rob has published numerous technical articles on the web and in print, and is a Microsoft MVP in ASP.NET.

Steph: What makes a blog successful according to you? Is it traffic, reach, revenue, etc.?

Rob: It's easy to focus on traffic, and historically that's what I've used to measure success. But in my case the real metric is the amount of consulting work I am able to generate. Nearly all of my leads over the past 18 months have come through my blog, either from subscribers or indirectly through search engines. Being able to sustain and grow a software consulting business based on this source is quite a testament to the power of a niche audience.

Steph: When did you decide you finally reached success with your blog?

Rob: About 12 months ago I realized that the hundreds of hours I had invested were beginning to pay off. This was the point where I stopped all other marketing efforts and began to rely solely on customers contacting me through my blog. I thought it was a fluke at first, but it just keeps growing.

Steph: How long does it take to become a successful blogger?

Rob: It took around 500 hours over the course of 15 months to work out the kinks in my writing, learn what my audiences likes, and build a following.

Steph: Who do you think are the most successful bloggers on the internet today?

Rob: Joel Spolsky (**http://www.JoelOnSoftware.com**) and Seth Godin (**http://sethgodin.typepad.com/**). Both have built multi-million dollar businesses around their blogs. They make no money directly from their blogs, but monetize them through their products, websites, books, and speaking engagements.

Steph: Which five blogs do you regularly read?

Rob:

Joel Spolsky's Joel on Software (**http://www.JoelOnSoftware.com**)—I've been a dedicated reader since 2001.

Aaron Wall's SEO Book (**http://www.seobook.com/blog**)—The best SEO blog.

Jeff Atwood's Coding Horror (**http://www.codinghorror.com/blog/**)—Not only a brilliant guy, but a gifted writer.

Bob Walsh's 47 hats (**http://47hats.com/**)—One of the authorities on small software companies.

Scott Hanselman's Hanselminutes Podcast (**http://www.hanselminutes.com/**)—A podcast rather than a blog. Every episode teaches me something, even the ones I don't think I'm going to like.

Steph: Which websites would you recommend for any new bloggers starting to blog?

Rob:

Copyblogger (**http://www.copyblogger.com/**)

Pearsonified (**http://www.pearsonified.com/**)

Seth's Blog (**http://sethgodin.typepad.com/**)

Micro Persuasion (**http://www.micropersuasion.com/**)

Steph: Which book(s) would you recommend for new bloggers (these can range from marketing books, blogging books, etc.)?

Rob: I haven't read any books about blogging due to the wealth of information available online. I think you could stay busy for the next few years absorbing the blogging and marketing information freely available on the web.

Steph: What is your most successful blog post ever?

Rob: By a narrow margin it's Nine Things Developers Want More Than Money (**http://www.softwarebyrob.com/2006/10/31/nine-things-developers-want-more-than-money/**). This post hit the front page of Digg and had around 50,000 views in the first three days. Since publication it's had close to 150,000 views.

Steph: What's your biggest tip on writing a successful blog post?

Rob: Write a good headline, but deliver on your content.

If you look at Nine Things Developers Want More Than Money, you'll notice it's thoroughly researched and covers the topic from several angles with a lot of detail. I went through at least 6 drafts of this post and I'm still happy with how it turned out (I can't say that for all of posts).

I read a lot of social news sites, and nothing is more frustrating than clicking on a killer headline where the article doesn't actually say anything. Headlines are important, but you have to have something to back them up.

Steph: What's your best advice in regards to content and writing for bloggers?

Rob: For me it's been all about practice. Many of my early posts are not that great, and looking back I polished a lot of rough edges when my blog had only a few hundred readers. This was good—getting to the front page of Digg with a bad article is pointless. You'll garner some traffic but no one will stick around and you'll earn a reputation for bad content.

Steph: How important do you think are the headlines of your blog articles?

Rob: Extremely important. A good portion of my traffic comes from social news sites such as Digg, Del.icio.us, and Reddit. On these sites an amazing article with a bad headline will get you nowhere. I have several posts, especially early on, that fit this description. A good headline and a bad article will provide traffic, but you won't retain any of them as subscribers. A good headline is critical, but a good article is also important.

Steph: Do you spend any money and time on marketing?

Rob: I don't spend any money on marketing. I do submit relevant posts to a few social news sites if readers don't beat me to it.

Steph: What are your main methods of marketing your blog?

Rob: Social news sites, organic search.

Steph: Which marketing tactic has surprised you the most in terms of its effectiveness?

Rob: As my blog aged and came out of the Google Sandbox. I had no idea how much traffic I would receive from organic search queries. During some months up to one-third of my traffic comes from organic search.

The Google Sandbox is a filter affect that Google places on new websites to stop them from ranking high for competitive keywords. The thought is that the longer a website has been around, the more authority it has. I've heard estimates of the sandbox duration from 18 months to 2 years, which fits my experience.

Steph: What are your quick and short five best tips for blogging?

Rob:

Write—This almost goes without saying, but you are going to have to get the bad writing out of your system before you can get into the good stuff. Get started as soon as you can, even if you never publish it.

Read Other Blogs—Know what the other bloggers in your community are talking about and if you have something to say, add to the conversation. I've found that crossing community boundaries (e.g. from software development to marketing) doesn't work so well, since bringing marketing people to a software blog doesn't result in new subscriptions.

Publish Weekly—Many blog marketing guides will tell you to publish daily (or more). I've found this overloads my readers, and that I spend too much time writing bad posts to fill this unrealistic quota. 1-2 well-written posts per week has been my sweet spot.

Learn Basic SEO—Until you know basic search engine optimization you will be missing out on a good source of free traffic. Learn how to find keywords to target, how to use meta descriptions for pretty search engine summary displays, and how to configure your blog to maximize each post's search engine ranking.

Buy an existing website—When starting a new blog you will be in the Google Sandbox for 18-24 months (see above for a definition of the Google Sandbox). Instead of starting from scratch, look on Sitepoint for an existing website or blog that you can purchase. If you are serious about blogging, the money you spend will more than pay for itself by allowing you to begin ranking in Google immediately.

Steph: What is the most common pitfall new bloggers generally fall into?

Rob: Publishing short posts devoid of original content. Don't publish just to increase your post count. There are popular blogs that do this better than you can hope to, so find your niche and write original material. If you don't have a backlog of original ideas to write about you should seriously consider whether you want to start a blog.

Steph: If you knew what you know now when you first started, what's the one biggest tip you'd give yourself today?

Rob: Use WordPress as your blogging engine. I recently migrated to WordPress, and not only is it an amazing piece of software, but the community surrounding it provides plugins for everything you could imagine.

Steph: What repels you the most from a blog (animations, in your face advertising, etc.)?

Rob: I have real trouble reading bad writing. I can handle typos and even a few misspellings, but a good idea that's poorly expressed is enough to send me packing.

Steph: Do you make any direct money from your blog through advertising, product placements, etc.?

Rob: I don't. I tried Google AdSense and FeedBurner's RSS Ads, but together they brought in under $20 per month, which to me is not worth the clutter.

I do include my Amazon Affiliate code when I link to Amazon, and have made a few hundred dollars from that over the past couple years.

Steph: What is your best monetization method (Ads, affiliate marketing, etc.)?

Rob: Monetization for me is consulting clients.

Steph: Do you find you get more from direct monetization of your blog or from opportunities that come because of the existence of your blog?

Rob: Hands down from consulting opportunities that come to me through my blog.

Steph: What's your most interesting story related to your blog and blogging experience?

Rob: I received an email from a major publishing house asking if I was interested in writing a book. I don't have time right now, but I'm putting it on my list for the future.

Steph: What's the one biggest opportunity that came to you because of your blog?

Rob: Being able to run a consulting firm that can focus on doing great work (instead of spending gobs of time on marketing) has been my biggest opportunity.

Steph: Thank you Rob for the interview.

Chapter 35

Rohit Bhargava

Influential Marketing Blog

http://rohitbhargava.typepad.com/

Rohit leads the interactive marketing team at Ogilvy Public Relations Worldwide and is a founding member of the pioneering Digital Influence Group. He publishes the award winning Influential Marketing blog and has been featured in dozens of publications worldwide including The Wall Street Journal, BusinessWeek, and Fast Company. He is the author of a book focused on the necessity of putting personality into marketing entitled Personality Not Included.

Steph: What makes a blog successful according to you? Is it traffic, reach, revenue, etc.?

Rohit: For my blog, I never really looked at it as a moneymaker. I don't run ads or worry too much about unique page views. My focus has always been on reach, because my blog is a way of extending my personal brand. If I can get more people reading my blog, whether they physically read it on my site, through RSS feeds, or get my content through it being syndicated onto another site, then that's fine. The power of blogging is that you can have your voice travel far beyond the people that you physically meet or have the chance to interact with. That's a pretty potent idea.

Steph: When did you decide you finally reached success with your blog?

Rohit: I think it came down to two things. The first was when I started getting a lot of media requests for interviews as a result of the blog. The second, and more important moment in my eyes was when I heard from some new bloggers that my blog had inspired them to start blogging too.

Steph: How long does it take to become a successful blogger?

Rohit: 67 days, but to quote one of my favorite disclaimers...your results may vary. Actually, there isn't really a single number for how long it takes, because ultimately it comes down to how you are judging being successful.

Steph: Who do you think are the most successful bloggers on the internet today?

Rohit: Again, success comes down to what you are trying to do. By any measure, I think Dooce is one of the most financially successful blog stories out there...where Heather was able to start supporting her whole family from her blog.

Steph: Which five blogs do you regularly read?

Rohit: This will probably seem odd, but the way I tend to read blogs is in spurts. There aren't really any blogs I read "regularly"...because with my travel schedule I don't always have time to do that. When I do read them, I tend to catch up on lots of old posts and many blogs at the same time.

Steph: Which websites would you recommend for any new bloggers starting to blog?

Rohit: For new bloggers, I think it's important to find your voice and the type of blog that you want to have. For that reason, I would say you should try and read blogs with a variety of different styles. Here are a few that I would recommend:

Web Strategy by Jeremiah Owyang (**http://www.web-strategist.com/blog/**)

Adrants by Steve Hall (**http://www.adrants.com/**)

How to Change the World by Guy Kawasaki (**http://blog.guykawasaki.com/**)

Seth Godin's Blog (**http://sethgodin.typepad.com/**)

Logic + Emotion by David Armano (**http://darmano.typepad.com/**)

Steph: Which book(s) would you recommend for new bloggers (these can range from marketing books, blogging books, etc.)?

Rohit: Not sure that these would be considered blogging books, but these would be at the top of my list for marketing books:

Citizen Marketers by Jackie Huba and Ben McConnell

Word of Mouth Marketing by Andy Sernovitz

Save the Cat by Blake Snyder

Anatomy of Buzz by Emanuel Rosen

Blink by Malcolm Gladwell

Steph: What is your most successful blog post ever?

Rohit: That would have to be my "5 Rules of Social Media Optimization" (http://rohitbhargava.typepad.com/weblog/2006/08/5_rules_of_soci.html). It sparked a new field of online marketing, was rated by Nielson as one of the top 100 most linked blog posts of 2006. Interestingly, it's been just over a year and I still get links to the post and occasional new translations of it in new languages.

Steph: What's your biggest tip on writing a successful blog post?

Rohit: I think the biggest tip I could offer is that you always need to offer an original idea and point of view. That and a great title. Headlines matter when you're blogging...so think like a copywriter and come up with something people can't help clicking.

Steph: What's your best advice in regards to content and writing for bloggers?

Rohit: See above—it's all about offering something insightful in your posts.

Steph: How important do you think are the headlines of your blog articles?

Rohit: Super important. Always have a great headline.

Steph: Do you spend any money and time on marketing?

Rohit: As much time as I can spare, no money.

Steph: What are your main methods of marketing your blog?

Rohit: My main method would be direct contact with other influential bloggers when I post something that I think they would be interested in. Directly emailing links to your blog, submitting it to social networks or social bookmarking sites, and sharing your posts on social networks are all great ways of marketing your blog...as long as you are sharing something relevant.

Steph: Which marketing tactic has surprised you the most in terms of its effectiveness?

Rohit: Passive marketing has been the most surprising for me in terms of how well it works. For example, you know that when you send a link to someone you are doing something directly. But now I can post an update on Twitter, or add a link to del.icio.us and people will see that and comment on it or send me something that relates to it. It's like using your thoughts for marketing.

Steph: What are your quick and short five best tips for blogging?

Rohit:

Set a realistic target—this keeps you from burning out or suffering from "blog guilt." My target has always been a minimum of 3 posts per week.

Share insights—there are too many links blogs that are just sharing things already out there. You need to add value.

Always collect ideas—I keep a running list of ideas and add to it anytime anything inspires me. Many of those never turn into posts, but it keeps me from ever having to stare at a blank screen when writing a post.

Figure out how to half write—I use half-writing all the time. It's a way for me to get the essence of an idea out, but keep the post handy so I can finish it later. You'd be amazed how much easier blogging can seem if you don't have the pressure on yourself to finish a post or make it perfect

Learn the 25 styles of blogging—I published a presentation introducing the 25 core style of blogging (**http://rohitbhargava.typepad.com/weblog/2007/04/the_25_basic_st.html**). It's a great resource for any new blogger and the link is included at the end of this section.

Note: These tips are excerpted from my blog post called "How to Find Time to Blog (When It's Not Your Day Job) at **http://rohitbhargava.typepad.com/weblog/2007/07/how-to-find-tim.html**

Steph: What is the most common pitfall new bloggers generally fall into?

Rohit: I think that any new blogger today will likely have other bloggers that they look up to and read on a consistent basis. The biggest pitfall I have seen for many bloggers is to try too hard to be like their idols. The greatest thing you can do is to find your own voice and made it distinctly yours rather than trying to copy someone else's.

Steph: If you knew what you know now when you first started, what's the one biggest tip you'd give yourself today?

Rohit: One tip would definitely be to choose the right URL. My blog has most of its links at the current address which is a subdomain of Typepad. I have my own URL, but the links are not aggregated between them. My other tip would be to just jump into blogging and start your blog even if you may not be sure what you will write about. When I started blogging, I thought my blog would be about user interfaces. If you look at my first few posts, they were just on that. But I ended up rebranding and focusing more on interactive marketing. After about 2 years, I rebranded again to take the word "interactive" out of the title of my blog and just call it "Influential Marketing."

Steph: What repels you the most from a blog (animations, in your face advertising, etc.)?

Rohit: I can usually see past those things if the content is great. The problem is, many of the blogs that are too focused on making money end up compromising on great content and when the site is not as useful, I tend not to return.

Steph: Do you make any direct money from your blog through advertising, product placements, etc.?

Rohit: No direct advertising money, though I have had several offers to test products that relate to what I have written about and accept these offers on occasion. In the cases where I do, it's important to me that I disclose what I have accepted and why.

Steph: What is your best monetization method (Ads, affiliate marketing, etc.)?

Rohit: There is no single best. I think being part of the Blogher network works great for some bloggers, Google Adwords work better for others. I like the idea of microsponsorships on blogs (which is something I have written about in the past) and am considering adding something like that to my blog.

Steph: Do you find you get more from direct monetization of your blog or from opportunities that come because of the existence of your blog?

Rohit: Definitely more benefit from opportunities that my blog opens up for me, of course I don't actually have any advertising so I don't have a way of comparing them.

Steph: What's your most interesting story related to your blog and blogging experience?

Rohit: The people I meet at events who know me from my blog always make for interesting stories. There was a moment also when a colleague of mine needed a liver transplant and only had a few days to live without one, so we launched a blogging effort to try and help spread awareness for organ donors and transplants. She got her liver and it was a big moment for us where we realized the real power of blogs to bring people together.

Steph: What's the one biggest opportunity that came to you because of your blog?

Rohit: I got my book deal with McGraw-Hill to publish my first book in part because of my blog. I did go the traditional route and got a great agent and then sold the deal, but the blog factored heavily into it. The book deal would have to be the biggest, followed by getting mentioned in the Wall Street Journal, and then a long list of media mentions and speaking requests as a result.

Steph: Any other comments or thoughts you'd like to share?

Rohit: Yes...Personality Not Included (my book) is coming out in March of 2008 in stores near you. Unless you live somewhere remote...in which case, just order it on Amazon.

Chapter
36

Seth Godin

http://sethgodin.typepad.com/

Seth Godin is a worldwide bestselling author of numerous books which have changed the way people think about marketing, change and work. His book, Permission Marketing, was an Amazon.com Top 100 bestseller for a year, a Fortune Best Business Book and spent four months on the Business Week bestseller list. It also appeared on the New York Times business book bestseller list.

Seth also wrote Unleashing the Ideavirus which is the most popular ebook ever written. More than 1,000,000 people downloaded the digital version of this book about how ideas spread. It's been featured in USA Today, The New York Times, The Industry Standard, and Wired Online. Ideavirus hit #4 on the Amazon Japan bestseller list, and #5 in the USA.

The Big Red Fez, Godin's book on web design, was the #1 ebook (worldwide) on Amazon for almost a year before it was published in paperback in 2002. The Miami Herald called it one of the best business books of the year.

Survival is Not Enough, another book written by Seth, has also made bestseller lists in Germany, the UK and the United States. And one of his latest books, Purple Cow (mentioned in several interviews throughout this book), was a New York Times and Wall Street Journal bestseller. It's all about how companies can transform themselves by becoming remarkable.

Seth is also a renowned speaker. He was recently chosen as one of 21 speakers for the Next Century by Successful Meetings and is consistently rated among the very best speakers by the audiences he addresses.

Seth was the founder and CEO of Yoyodyne, the industry's leading interactive direct marketing company, which Yahoo! acquired in late 1998.

[Disclaimer: Some of the interview questions answered here are extracted from Seth's blog with his explicit permission.]

Steph: What makes a blog successful according to you? Is it traffic, reach, revenue, etc.?

Seth: To achieve success now you can't be invisible, you must be remarkable. That means your blog must have attributes that cause people to remark about them. One person tells another and so on, spreading the word until millions of people are clamoring to have whatever it is you're offering.

What is true is that we often know success when it smashes us in the face. We didn't "know it" when Google went public at $85 a share (did you buy shares with your house as collateral?) but we sure knew it when it hit $300.

Steph: When did you decide you finally reached success with your blog? And how does someone go about achieving success like you?

Seth: We all want to open big. We want our product launches to be instant successes. We want the resumes we send out to be opened in one day, a call the next, an interview the third and a corner office by the end of the week.

When I first started many years ago, my readership was tiny. Just a few people a day. Today, they say this is one of the top 100 most-visited blogs in the English language... and I hear from people I never imagined I'd run into again (if I taught you canoeing in 1978, sure, send me an email!)

Permission Marketing : Turning Strangers Into Friends And Friends Into Customers a book I wrote seven years ago just went back to press at the publisher and continues to sell. Unleashing the Ideavirus, which you can get for free online or in a handy paperback edition, came out five years ago... but they're just now launching trade organizations around the ideas in it.

The bottom line is that it's way way easier to start things than it used to be (opening a movie big costs a tenth of a billion dollars, while opening a blog costs about twenty). The natural, user-driven networks that make a product succeed or fail rarely hit all at once. But the snowball effect online is far more powerful than the old-world scream & dream approach.

So, what's it mean to you?

Make something worth making.

Sell something worth talking about.

Believe in what you do because you may have to do it for a long time before it catches on.

Don't listen to the first people who give you feedback.

Don't give up. Not for a while, anyway.

Steph: Which websites would you recommend for any new bloggers starting to blog?

Seth: Have you ever recommended a doctor?

On what basis?

Did you do an analysis of the outcomes of his treatments along a wide range of patients and compare those outcomes to similar doctors in the same community?

Or was it based on his bedside manner or even how polite his receptionist was?

And what about the accounting firm or law firm or personal trainer you were talking about the other day?

Is it possible that people recommend a Mac so often because of things that having nothing to do with a side-by-side analysis of the speed of data entry in Word?

All a rhetorical way of pointing out that businesses (and people) do two things. Most of focus on just one (at least when we're doing the task at hand) which is the task at hand. But, there's something else that's far more important, something disconnected from what's produced but certainly related: how you made the customer feel.

How's this for a 98% rule: *By a factor of three, what you do is not nearly as important as how it makes people feel.*

If you buy that, then the question is this: why do you spend almost all your time on the wrong thing?

Steph: For the other interviews in this book, I've been asking everyone which book(s) they recommend but in your case since you've written so many, I'd rather just list them. Not only are the books you've written great, but many of the other bloggers have suggested them.

Books written by Seth:

The Dip: A Little Book That Teaches You When to Quit (and When to Stick)

Meatball Sundae: Is Your Marketing out of Sync?

Small Is the New Big: and 183 Other Riffs, Rants, and Remarkable Business Ideas

Permission Marketing : Turning Strangers Into Friends And Friends Into Customers

All Marketers Are Liars: The Power of Telling Authentic Stories in a Low-Trust World

Purple Cow

Unleashing the Ideavirus

The Big Red Fez: How To Make Any Web Site Better

Survival Is Not Enough: Why Smart Companies Abandon Worry and Embrace Change

Free Prize Inside

Steph: What is your most successful blog post ever?

Seth: Understanding the meaning of "successful" is critical. I've had posts on the music industry and on blog popularity that have received hundreds of thousands of unique visits. But for me, a successful post is not necessarily a popular one. Mass is not the objective. So, I guess my most successful post is the one that changed any given reader in a way that they viewed as helpful.

Steph: What's your biggest tip on writing a successful blog post?

Seth:

Use lists.

Be topical...write posts that need to be read right now.

Learn enough to become the expert in your field.

Break news.

Be timeless...write posts that will be readable in a year.

Be among the first with a great blog on your topic, then encourage others to blog on the same topic.

Share your expertise generously so people recognize it and depend on you.

Announce news.

Write short, pithy posts.

Write stuff that people want to read and share.

Steph: How important do you think are the headlines of your blog articles?

Seth: You get judged by your headline or your layout, or the first line of your press release or the first beats of your riff. If the smartmob can't figure out your story in two seconds, they ignore it or they make up their own.

If you want to please everyone, it helps to be clear, obvious and direct. And safe and predictable as well.

Of course, if you try to make it clear to everyone, the chances of having your story spread in the long run go down. Because direct is often not so interesting, especially to sneezers. And doesn't always involve the joy of discovery.

So perhaps, the best strategy is to be a bit less obvious, a bit indirect, telling a story you can live with because it's true, but a story that might take more than a minute to understand.

Steph: What is the most common pitfall new bloggers generally fall into?

Seth: The mistake most blogs and books make: *they are about the writer, not the reader.*

Years ago, a friend (a former judge) wrote a thriller. It was based on a true story that actually happened to him. It was terrible. Why? The fact that it had actually happened was interesting to him, but the typical reader didn't care at all. That's because the typical reader didn't know him.

The things that fascinate you about your life are almost always banal to strangers. Strangers want to read about their lives, not yours. And guess what? The same thing is true about prospects and customers and just about anything you can imagine marketing.

Steph: If you knew what you know now when you first started, what's the one biggest tip you'd give yourself today?

Seth: Own the domain of your blog, and show up on every social media service you can handle.

Steph: What repels you the most from a blog (animations, in your face advertising, etc.)?

Seth: Don't write about your cat, your boyfriend or your kids. Don't be boring.

Steph: What's your most interesting story related to your blog and blogging experience?

Seth: Once, exactly once, I got a better table at a restaurant as a result. That, and the guys at Headblade that make razors for bald guys... they sent me a razor once.

Steph: Thank you for answering the interview questions Seth.

Chapter 37

Stephane Grenier

Follow Steph

http://www.FollowSteph.com

Stephane founded LandlordMax Software Inc in 2003, a company specialized in selling property management software to real estate investors, property management companies, banks, and cities. Since its beginnings LandlordMax has continued to grow, with sales in almost every continent of the world.

In 2005, Stephane started his blog FollowSteph.com to give his customers more transparency into the inner working of his company and himself. Originally the blog mainly focused on real estate and LandlordMax itself, but this quickly evolved to publishing articles about how to run a business, be successful, and of course a view behind the scenes of his company. On the blog he shares with his audience not only the successes of his company, but also the experiences and adventures he's had in business. The blog is now generating approximately half a million unique visitors a year and growing exponentially.

Before founding his company, Stephane was primarily a consultant for IT companies across Canada and the United States. He's worked mainly with enterprise level applications in many roles such as lead developer, team lead, project lead, etc., with the largest website handling over 50 million unique visitors a year.

With a BSc in Computer Science, he has spoken at seminars on how to generate traffic for companies and websites. He is an active member of a local passive income investment group, often speaking about his latest experiences.

Steph: What makes a blog successful according to you? Is it traffic, reach, revenue, etc.?

Stephane: Overall a blog is successful if it has reach, if it has some traffic and some impact on people's lives.

Whether or not a blog has revenues is not as important to me. In any case, revenues, or opportunities, usually come as a by-product of reach.

Steph: When did you decide you finally reached success with your blog?

Stephane: When people started to link to my articles and when some of my articles received a lot of comments. But more noticeably, when my company's revenues started to increase because of my transparency about it on the blog. It was significant within a very short time. Beyond the obvious, the traffic coming from the search engines, my blog is the site that sends the most traffic to my company's website, more than even paid advertising!

Steph: How long does it take to become a successful blogger?

Stephane: It takes time and commitment. Some people can achieve it quickly, but on average I would suggest at least a year or two. It takes some time for people to notice you, for you to get your rhythm going, for you to really understand what blogging is all about. I've been blogging for two years and I'm still very much growing as a blogger.

The key to remember is that it's not a sprint. I've seen so many people start blogging only to stop within a few months. It's very similar to when people go to the gym as a New Year's Resolution. New bloggers are very eager early on and push very hard. They post daily, if not more. Then after a week or so, the posting frequency starts to slow down. All of a sudden it becomes once a week, then once a month. Then you see the famous "Sorry I haven't posted in a while but..." post. Success takes time, plan for it.

Steph: Who do you think are the most successful bloggers on the internet today?

Stephane: Unfortunately after having conducted all the interviews for this book my view is skewed. But I have to say Darren Rowse from Problogger (**http://www.ProBlogger.net**) is near the top, if not at the very top. Almost everyone I interviewed mentioned him in their interviews! That's amazing. No one else was so consistently measured. Many other people were mentioned several times, but no one else was mentioned on almost every single interview. I've also been reading his blog daily for as long as I can remember, back to when it was .net and not .com. It's a great resource to learn how to blog.

Steph: Which five blogs do you regularly read?

Stephane: I follow over 100 blog feeds. So although I asked this question to everyone, it's a hard one for me to answer... But if I had to take a stab at it (focusing mainly on those with wider appeal), I would say:

Problogger (**http://www.Problogger.net**)

Coding Horror (**http://www.CodingHorror.com**)

The Daily WTF (**http://www.TheDailyWTF.com**)

Joel On Software (**http://www.JoelOnSoftware.com**)

Successful Software (**http://www.SuccessfulSoftware.net**)

Create Passionate Users (**http://headrush.typepad.com/creating_passionate_users/**)

CopyBlogger (**http://www.CopyBlogger.com**)

It's very hard for me to stop here. I read so many other great blogs such as Seth Godin's, Retro Blog, Courtney Tuttle's, etc. Like I said, I try to keep up with over 100 different blogs, all of them great.

Steph: Which websites would you recommend for any new bloggers starting to blog?

Stephane: If you want to read blogs about how to blog, you definitely want to check out the following:

Problogger (**http://www.Problogger.net**)

ShoeMoney (**http://www.ShoeMoney.com**)

John Chow (**http://www.JohnChow.com**)

CopyBlogger (**http://www.CopyBlogger.com**)

Lorelle on WordPress (**http://lorelle.wordpress.com/**)

Steph: Which book(s) would you recommend for new bloggers (these can range from marketing books, blogging books, etc.)?

Stephane: Since I started writing this book I've learned of several new books I'd like to read, such as Clear Blogging. But since I haven't read it, I can't yet recommend it. Therefore of those I've read, I'd recommend:

On Writing Well

How to Win Friends and Influence People

Maximum Influence

22 Immutable Laws of Branding

Call to Action

Don't Make Me Think

Getting Everything You Can Out of All You've Got

Founders at Work

Growing a Business

And anything by Seth Godin on marketing, at least early on in your blogging career when marketing takes up a bigger portion of your time.

Steph: What is your most successful blog post ever?

Stephane: That's hard to say. I've had several posts that have garnered a lot of traffic and comments, and still continue to do so. My most successful posts are probably:

7 Simple Tips And 5 Secrets to Increase Your Credit Score (**http://www.followsteph.com/2005/12/13/7-simple-tips-and-5-secrets-to-increase-your-credit-score/**)

Windows Vista Read-Only (**http://www.followsteph.com/2007/06/17/windows-vista-read-only/**)

A Large Monitor is Actually Cheaper Than a Small Monitor (**http://www.followsteph.com/2006/12/19/a-large-monitor-is-actually-cheaper-than-a-small-monitor/**)

How to Write Out Your Domain Name (**http://www.followsteph.com/2007/07/12/how-to-write-out-your-domain-name/**)

LandlordMax's Most Challenging Bug (**http://www.followsteph.com/2006/10/19/landlordmaxs-most-challenging-bug/**)

Steph: What's your biggest tip on writing a successful blog post?

Stephane: Try to write something you'd like to read from a stranger. The key is "*from a stranger*". This means no writing about your dog or cat. Write about what other people care about. Give them something of value. Share your knowledge in a way that can benefit others.

Steph: What's your best advice in regards to content and writing for bloggers?

Stephane: Firstly, give value. Write something that people will want to read and that they can apply.

Secondly, you need to continually work on improving your writing. Try and test things. Read books about writing. Look at the style of others. Find what works for you and what doesn't. Basically always try to improve your writing, everyone can. I know I sure can.

Above that, think about using images on your blog. Especially emotionally charged images. I've used images in the past, but in the last while I've been conscientiously putting an image at the top of almost every article I write. The results have been nothing short of amazing. If you don't have pictures, don't worry, there are lots of great places to get affordable stock photos for your blog such as Stockxpert (**http://www.stockxpert.com**), iStockphoto (**http://www.iStockphoto.com**), etc.

Steph: How important do you think are the headlines of your blog articles?

Stephane: Very! I asked this very question in the interviews because I wanted to confirm the importance of headlines, especially as your blog grows a very large audience. And it appears so.

Steph: Do you spend any money and time on marketing?

Stephane: I definitely spend both time and money on marketing and advertising for my company. For my blog I did spend both, but these days it's mostly time. And even that is starting to dwindle. I now mainly focus on improving the quality of my content. I've found that once I reached a critical mass, I got a better return on my time improving my writing and articles than marketing my blog.

Steph: What are your main methods of marketing your blog?

Stephane: In the past I use to actively apply certain marketing tactics. Today I guess I still do, but it's no longer conscientious. Those I remember actively using are:

Comment on other blogs

Comment on discussion forums. Participate in discussions

Link to other relevant articles on your blog

Add your URL to your signature on emails, discussion forums, etc.

Tell people about your blog.

Send emails/tips to prominent bloggers about your better articles

Focus on SEO (I no longer really do this)

Avoid writing negative comments about others, especially scathing comments. Look for something positive, you'll usually find it. And if you have nothing positive to say, think about writing about something else.

Steph: Which marketing tactic has surprised you the most in terms of its effectiveness?

Stephane: The ongoing value of getting an article showcased on a prominent blog. For example, early on I had a post titled "7 Simple Tips And 5 Secrets to Increase Your Credit Score" (**http://www.followsteph.com/2005/12/13/7-simple-tips-and-5-secrets-to-increase-your-credit-score/**) which was linked from LifeHacker.com (**http://lifehacker.com/software/credit/increase-your-credit-score-143393.php**). This one write-up continues to send me decent traffic, even 2 years later!

Steph: What are your quick and short five best tips for blogging?

Stephane:

Get your own domain. Once you've established a blog there's nothing worse than having to move the URL. Not only will you lose some of your traffic, you'll also lose most of your search engine rankings.

Use pictures, especially those which exude emotions, for your articles. It's great to set the mood of the article. One of my articles, "Why do Some Projects Continue to Push Unrealistic Software Development Schedules?" (**http://www.followsteph.com/2008/01/14/why-do-some-projects-continue-to-push-unrealistic-software-development-schedules/**) started with the picture of someone panicking holding a clock. Now that's setting a mood.

Write about things your audience can benefit from, assuming they're strangers.

Come up with your own topics. Be original. Don't just be reactionary, come up with new articles, angles, etc.

Link freely to relevant articles and sources. I personally love finding related links on blog articles that I read. It lets me go beyond the article I'm reading, I can't even begin to count the number of bloggers I've met by either them linking to my website or vice versa. Contacts I wouldn't have made otherwise.

Steph: What is the most common pitfall new bloggers generally fall into?

Stephane: Bloggers who mainly focus on themselves and their personal lives. Maybe if we personally knew you we'd be interested, but overall we're generally more interested in "what's in it for me". So give us something of value and we'll keep coming back.

Another pitfall is the "I'm sorry I haven't posted in a while but..." post. Don't give us an excuse, just do it. Just write.

Long winded articles is another pitfall. In the book, "On Writing Well", the author states it best "Don't say you were a bit confused and sort of tired and a little depressed and somewhat annoyed. Be confused. Be tired. Be depressed. Be annoyed. Don't hedge your prose with little timidities. Good writing is lean and confident".

Another common pitfall is when people don't have an opinion. Be about something. Right or wrong, take a side. Give your opinion. State something. I might not agree, but I'll listen to your arguments. Ever wonder why Don Cherry (a Canadian hockey commentator) is so successful when a lot of people don't like him? Because he's got an opinion and he's not afraid to state it.

Steph: If you knew what you know now when you first started, what's the one biggest tip you'd give yourself today?

Stephane: Write lean and mean. Don't blah blah. This is still something I'm really working on, but I hope I'm getting better.

Steph: What repels you the most from a blog (animations, in your face advertising, etc.)?

Stephane: My biggest pet peeve is an over abundance of ads. It's ok to have ads, I have them too. The key is that they shouldn't take over your blog, they should just flow with the blog. Maybe you won't get as many click-throughs or what have you, but that's ok. The increase in traffic will offset it.

Steph: Do you make any direct money from your blog through advertising, product placements, etc.?

Stephane: I make money from my blog in several ways. The biggest and most profitable way is through the increased sales of my company's software because of the transparency I give. That eclipses all other revenues.

After that I've gotten a few licenses for reviewing higher end software that we use at LandlordMax. Of course every product I've reviewed is used at LandlordMax, and I gave very honest reviews.

Afterwards I make a little revenue from Adsense, Text-Link-Ads, etc. The remainder is from affiliate marketing, from affiliates like Amazon. Every time I refer a book or a product that's available from Amazon, I try to include a link. It isn't much in comparison, but it continues to scale up over time. There's definitely a long-tail effect there.

Steph: What is your best monetization method (Ads, affiliate marketing, etc.)?

Stephane: I guess I just answered that in my previous answer.

Steph: Do you find you get more from direct monetization of your blog or from opportunities that come because of the existence of your blog?

Stephane: By far the best return has been the increase in sales of my company's product LandlordMax. The transparency has been great.

Something I'll just mention as an aside, not only does the blog increase the transparency but it also helps with technical support. For example, there are many times when a link to a full article is better than anything we can say in an email because the blog article will go in more detail than we could on a support request. A great example of this is why we don't offer phone support (**http://www.followsteph.com/2006/10/10/is-technical-phone-support-a-viable-option-for-a-software-company/**).

Steph: What's your most interesting story related to your blog and blogging experience?

Stephane: Probably my most interesting story was when I was talking to someone about the difference between HelpSpot and FogBugz for technical support versus project management and I mentioned an article I had written about it (**http://www.followsteph.com/2006/06/20/helpspot-versus-fogbugz/**). He remembered reading something similar about it, but couldn't remember the exact source. Well we quickly looked it up online, and lo and behold, it was indeed my article he had read and was referencing without knowing it!

Steph: What's the one biggest opportunity that came to you because of your blog?

Stephane: By far this book! If it wasn't for my blog I doubt I would have been able to generate the interest I did. I'm sure my blog created much of the credibility I needed to get such amazing and highly prominent bloggers to accept being interviewed for this book. Not only that, but having been blogging for over two years proved I knew what I was doing, and that it would be worth their time.

Steph: Any other comments or thoughts you'd like to share?

Stephane: Just do it! Most people never get beyond the idea stage, that is they never execute on their idea and just keep thinking what they're going to do. They research and research, they think and think, they analyze and analyze. Basically they get "analysis paralysis". They just don't execute. They never really take that first step towards execution, they just stay in the world of thinking and planning. Execution is the key. Execution is by far the hardest and most time consuming aspect of any endeavor, which is why it's usually where people stall. Ideas are a dime a dozen. Execution is the key. Just do it! Or as a good friend of mine likes to say, "Just throw a dart and start!"

Chapter 38

Steve Rubel

Micro Persuasion

http://www.micropersuasion.com/

Steve Rubel is a digital marketer with over 15 years experience. He currently serves as senior vice president in Edelman's me2revolution practice, the world's largest independent PR firm. He's charged with helping Edelman clients identify key insights, trends and emerging digital platforms that can be applied in marketing programs. He explores these topics on Micro Persuasion and in a bi-weekly column for AdAge Digital.

Steve is also a speaker and appears frequently in the press. He has been named to several prestigious lists, including: The Forbes.com Web Celeb 25, PC Magazine's 100 Favorite Blogs, Media Magazine's Media 100, the AlwaysOn/Technorati Open Media 100 and the CNET News.com Blog 100.

Steph: What makes a blog successful according to you? Is it traffic, reach, revenue, etc.?

Steve: None of the above. While there are certainly some blogs that are measured this way, no two are alike. Some bloggers simply want to find others who are like them online and be able to forge connections. So the metrics will really vary depending on what the blogger's goals are.

Steph: When did you decide you finally reached success with your blog?

Steve: In my case, I was hoping to build relationships with others who were passionate about how the web was changing business. So success came early —when I began to interact with people who were smarter than me on this subject.

Steph: How long does it take to become a successful blogger?

Steve: Again, it really depends. As little as a day to as much as a year if someone is trying to hone in on revenue opps.

Steph: Who do you think are the most successful bloggers on the internet today?

Steve: Nearly everyone who is using the medium for good.

Steph: Which five blogs do you regularly read?

Steve:

Scripting News (**http://www.scripting.com/**)

Blog Maverick (**http://www.blogmaverick.com/**)

Scobleizer (**http://scobleizer.com/**)

lifehacker (**http://lifehacker.com/**)

rexblog.com (**http://www.rexblog.com/**)

Steph: Which websites would you recommend for any new bloggers starting to blog?

Steve: Problogger.net is a great resource for people who are hoping to make money from blogging.

Steph: Which book(s) would you recommend for new bloggers (these can range from marketing books, blogging books, etc.)?

Steve:

Naked Conversations

Cluetrain Manifesto

The Long Tail

Steph: What is your most successful blog post ever?

Steve: Probably my series on Gmail (**http://tinyurl.com/2za7r9**). There are 400 links alone to the initial post.

Steph: What's your biggest tip on writing a successful blog post?

Steve: Be yourself. Know who you are, how you can add value and where—and where you can't.

Steph: What's your best advice in regards to content and writing for bloggers?

Steve: Blog for others, not yourself. In other words, create content that fills a void.

Steph: How important do you think are the headlines of your blog articles?

Steve: Incredibly—**http://nick.typepad.com/blog/2007/10/the-best-way-to.html**

Steph: Do you spend any money and time on marketing?

Steve: Well, I work in counseling companies on digital marketing. So in that sense, yes. In addition, my blog and various external activities help market the agency. However, beyond that I don't try to market the blog. It's been all organic.

Steph: What are your main methods of marketing your blog?

Steve: Basic stuff—offering full-text feed, providing high value content, good writing (at least I would like to think so).

Steph: Which marketing tactic has surprised you the most in terms of its effectiveness?

Steve: Blogs—when done right—are incredible SEO tools. I get 60 of my traffic through Google.

Steph: What are your quick and short five best tips for blogging?

Steve:

Blog your passions

Add value

Be brief

Use graphics and catchy headlines

Be a resource—find things that others don't see or have time to read

Steph: What is the most common pitfall new bloggers generally fall into?

Steve: Not being unique enough—if the goal is to get big and known. It's fine for personal blogs

Steph: If you knew what you know now when you first started, what's the one biggest tip you'd give yourself today?

Steve: Not to have swung to extremes. I was a proponent of too many technologies that are not going to have staying power. I would have been better off blogging about big trends as I do now.

Steph: What repels you the most from a blog (animations, in your face advertising, etc.)?

Steve: Poor content.

Steph: Do you make any direct money from your blog through advertising, product placements, etc.?

Steve: None—by choice. Edelman (my employer) has 1500 clients. So any attempt to make money this way could be in direct conflict with our business.

Steph: Do you find you get more from direct monetization of your blog or from opportunities that come because of the existence of your blog?

Steve: Without a doubt the two agencies I have worked for since I launched my blog in 2004 have benefitted. So, to me, the answer is the latter.

Steph: What's your most interesting story related to your blog and blogging experience?

Steve: My blog has helped me win several clients.

Steph: What's the one biggest opportunity that came to you because of your blog?

Steve: Press coverage—reams of it. Notably, a full-page photo in BusinessWeek a couple of years ago.

Steph: Any other comments or thoughts you'd like to share?

Steve: Nope, I think we covered it!

Trent Hamm

The Simple Dollar

http://www.thesimpledollar.com/

Trent Hamm is in his twenties, a father of two, and lives in rural Iowa. In April 2006 he went through what he calls a complete financial meltdown. This is when he threw himself head first into trying to figure out every nuance of fixing his financial situation, and after a few months he began to get the picture. Within eight months he had paid off all of his credit card debt, his vehicle, and also established an emergency fund. He then started The Simple Dollar in 2006 to share what he learned and help people who were struggling with similar issues.

Steph: What makes a blog successful according to you? Is it traffic, reach, revenue, etc.?

Trent: For me, success comes in the form of emails from readers who tell me that I have helped make positive changes in their life. In terms of comparing blogs, the top statistics I would look for are unbiased traffic statistics (SiteMeter, Quantcast, etc.) and subscribed RSS feed readers.

Steph: When did you decide you finally reached success with your blog?

Trent: When I started receiving emails fairly regularly from readers who had found inspiration in my blog and had used it to facilitate a turnaround in their life.

Steph: How long does it take to become a successful blogger?

Trent: I think it's more of a question of how long it takes to learn how to write consistently compelling posts that other people want to read. Once you figure that out—and the recipe is different for everyone—you'll find success no matter how you measure it.

Steph: Who do you think are the most successful bloggers on the internet today?

Trent: Those who write blogs that not only improve their own lives, but improve the lives of others.

Steph: Which five blogs do you regularly read?

Trent: It changes so much that it's hard to give a list of just five. I usually get obsessed with one blog, read almost the entire archives, then move on to another. I subscribe to about 600 blogs in my RSS reader.

Steph: Which websites would you recommend for any new bloggers starting to blog?

Trent: Google Reader. Subscribe to EVERY blog that interests you and read. Read a lot. Figure out what they do that makes you excited about them and interested in them.

Steph: Which book(s) would you recommend for new bloggers (these can range from marketing books, blogging books, etc.)?

Trent: "Made to Stick" by the Heath brothers and "Ogilvy on Advertising" have been the two most useful to me as a blogger.

Steph: What is your most successful blog post ever?

Trent: 30 Essential Pieces Of Free (and Open) Software for Windows (**http://www.thesimpledollar.com/2006/12/01/30-essential-pieces-of-free-and-open-software- for-windows/**)

Steph: What's your biggest tip on writing a successful blog post?

Trent: Try to take two ideas that are interesting on their own and combine them, usually in a framework that's easy to digest in little pieces. Here, I combined frugality and technology and made a list out of it.

Steph: What's your best advice in regards to content and writing for bloggers?

Trent: Before you even start writing, ask yourself honestly if you would have any interest in reading it. If the answer is no, you shouldn't be bothering with it.

Steph: How important do you think are the headlines of your blog articles?

Trent: Vital for getting outsiders on social bookmarking sites (like Digg, Reddit, del.icio.us, etc.) to read your post.

Steph: Do you spend any money and time on marketing?

Trent: Maybe fifteen minutes a week, and that's mostly in the form of seeing if I've had anything submitted on a social bookmarking site.

Steph: What are your main methods of marketing your blog?

Trent: Um... I keep tabs on Digg and reddit and see if I have anything that's been submitted. If I see something getting popular, I might upvote it. That's about it.

Steph: Which marketing tactic has surprised you the most in terms of its effectiveness?

Trent: Linking to other blogs in the natural course of my own posts, particularly smaller blogs. Quite often, they'll read your blog if they notice the link and if you're interesting, they'll link to you, too.

Steph: What are your quick and short five best tips for blogging?

Trent:

Write stuff you would want to read.

Spend almost all your time just thinking about and writing good content, not marketing.

Link to other blogs that you like frequently in your posts.

Keep a notebook and a pen in your pocket at all times to jot down inspirations.

Stick to a regular schedule so your readers will come back for more on a regular basis, too. If you're irregular, your readers will be as well.

Steph: What is the most common pitfall new bloggers generally fall into?

Trent: They write substandard stuff for a month, then give up when the world doesn't beat a path to their door. Your first 100 posts are your worst 100 posts, and most new bloggers haven't found their groove yet. Patience is what is needed early on.

Steph: If you knew what you know now when you first started, what's the one biggest tip you'd give yourself today?

Trent: Write fewer posts and make them better.

Steph: What repels you the most from a blog (animations, in your face advertising, etc.)?

Trent: Ads that interfere with reading the article in any way—mid-article ads basically mean I'm leaving the site immediately.

Steph: Do you make any direct money from your blog through advertising, product placements, etc.?

Trent: Yes, through direct ads.

Steph: What is your best monetization method (Ads, affiliate marketing, etc.)?

Trent: Google AdSense is my best money maker. Feedburner is second. Everything else trails far behind.

Steph: Do you find you get more from direct monetization of your blog or from opportunities that come because of the existence of your blog?

Trent: So far, directly from my blog. Other opportunities are just starting to really appear—they take much more time to build.

Steph: What's your most interesting story related to your blog and blogging experience?

Trent: I was in a bookstore browsing through personal finance books. A guy came in and picked up "Your Money or Your Life" and was reading the back of it. I just commented "I really like that book," and he said, "Yeah, I read about it online." I asked where he read about it and he referred to The Simple Dollar.

Steph: What's the one biggest opportunity that came to you because of your blog?

Trent: I was able to be involved in the ground floor of the development of a new online bank. Unfortunately, the subprime mortgage crisis caused the project to be nixed because the parent bank needed to consolidate their cash reserves.

Steph: Thank you for the interview Trent.

Chapter 40

Yaro Starak

Entrepreneur's Journey

http://www.entrepreneurs-journey.com/

Yaro Starak is a professional blogger, best known for www.Entrepreneurs-Journey.com, a blog that teaches people how to start a successful Internet business.

Although Yaro's never had a job, he's consistently made money online since his university days. In the last ten years he's run an English school, an online proofreading business, a freelance web development and hosting service, bought and sold websites for profit and has consulted on Internet businesses, both starting and growing them. Yaro even launched one of Australia's most popular sites dedicated to the trading card game, Magic: The Gathering, while traveling the world as a competitive player and tournament reporter for the game.

Today, Yaro is focused on his passion—blogging. He consistently earns over $6,000 per month from his blog and recently launched a new mentoring program (http://www.blogmastermind.com), to help others replicate his blogging success.

Yaro also published a guide on making money from blogs—The Blog Profits Blueprint—which you can download for free from http://www.blogmastermind.com/blueprint/

Steph: What makes a blog successful according to you? Is it traffic, reach, revenue, etc.?

Yaro: Success is determined by the motivation for creating the blog. If the owner has a certain goal and meets it, then I consider that a success.

However if you are looking at industry wide standards, traffic and exposure are the main criteria for a successful blog. Money counts too, but I think most people look at the number of readers and who you can influence as the most important factors.

Steph: When did you decide you finally reached success with your blog?

Yaro: Hmm, that's a tough question. My goals and aspirations keep changing. Originally I wanted to get to 500 daily readers by the end of my first year of blogging, but I made it to 1000, which was great.

I think for me though, the real realization that I had built something special was when I looked at my monthly blog earnings and realized I was making just as much from my blog as I was my other Internet business. At that point I felt I could stop doing everything else and just blog to make a living if I choose to. That was about the point where I was making around $3000 a month.

Steph: How long does it take to become a successful blogger?

Yaro: Given my previous responses you can imagine this question is quite variable too. People who are aiming for financial independence from blogging would say at the point where they can live off their blog earnings is the point of success.

Others might look at making their first blog post as successful.

Steph: Who do you think are the most successful bloggers on the internet today?

Yaro: The blogs that have gone super mainstream, such as:

Techcrunch (**http://www.techcrunch.com/**)

Engadget (**http://www.engadget.com/**)

Mashable (**http://mashable.com/**)

Lifehacker (**http://lifehacker.com/**)

Etc.

These blogs are larger than most print magazines and newspapers, which I think is an amazing achievement.

Steph: Which five blogs do you regularly read?

Yaro: You might be surprised to know that I rarely read blogs. I spend most of my time studying ebooks and audio from experts. I do pop into Darren's Problogger.net (**http://www.Problogger.net**) and several smaller Internet marketing blogs, but usually not for long.

I find the concentrated advice in information products much better than the shorter posts you find in blogs, plus I prefer to write to my own blog rather than read others.

In the past I have spent time at:

StevePavlina.com (**http://www.stevepavlina.com/blog/**)

JohnChow.com (**http://www.johnchow.com/**)

SEOMoz (**http://www.seomoz.org**)

Copyblogger (**http://www.copyblogger.com/**)

ChrisG (**http://www.chrisg.com/**)

AndyBeard (**http://andybeard.eu/**)

SEOBook (**http://www.seobook.com/**)

and several other blogs about Internet marketing, SEO, business and self development.

Steph: Which websites would you recommend for any new bloggers starting to blog?

Yaro: I have to plug my own resource first. My Blog Profits Blueprint free report

(**http://www.blogmastermind.com/blueprint/**) is a great starting point for any blogger wanting to get into making money from blogs.

By the time this interview comes out, my new project—becomeablogger.com (**http://www.becomeablogger.com**), should be ready too—which contains free videos to introduce people to blogging. This is a really good site, I'm quite proud of it and for any person who is very new to setting up a WordPress blog, becomeablogger.com is ideal—and free!

You can't not mention Problogger.net (**http://www.Problogger.net**) when talking blogging too, and there are many hundreds of other blogs that come up with great blogging advice now and then. None of them are quite as dedicated as Problogger, but there's lots to learn, so you should look around.

Steph: Which book(s) would you recommend for new bloggers (these can range from marketing books, blogging books, etc.)?

Yaro: If you are the kind of person who likes an all-in-one very basic beginners book, the Dummies Guide to blogging is a good starting point.

If you look online and search for "how to blog" you will find plenty of great free information too.

I think my answer to the previous question applies to this question as well.

Steph: What is your most successful blog post ever?

Yaro: Again, without defining success this is a challenging question. Personally I consider some of the major article series I have written as my best posts—

Is Professional Blogging A Sustainable Business Model? (**http://www.entrepreneurs-journey.com/616/professional-blogging-as-a-business-model/**)

The Sales Funnel Explained (**http://www.entrepreneurs-journey.com/691/the-sales-funnel-explained/**)

How I Make Money Online Series (**http://www.entrepreneurs-journey.com/200/making-money-online-part1/**)

How To Launch A Membership Site (**http://www.entrepreneurs-journey.com/773/how-to-launch-a-membership-site-part-1-build-your-preeminence/**)

In terms of raw financial return, any of the reviews in my blog archives are good choices as they each bring in a few thousand dollars a year for me.

Steph: What's your biggest tip on writing a successful blog post?

Yaro: Blog about topics you can discuss with authentic experience. Most bloggers get this wrong. You need to provide value and to provide value you have to know about things others do not and then explain it to them in an interesting manner. This is the key to powerful content.

Steph: What's your best advice in regards to content and writing for bloggers?

Yaro: The answer to the previous question is my very best advice regarding content and writing for bloggers. If you combine authentic content with a consistent posting frequency and a dash of marketing you have the formula for a successful blog.

Steph: How important do you think are the headlines of your blog articles?

Yaro: Headlines are absolutely critical. If you don't do a good job with your headline then the rest of your article is a waste because no one will read it.

Steph: Do you spend any money and time on marketing?

Yaro: I spend both money and time. Most of my marketing today is by giving away free information in reports and newsletters and of course from my blog.

I also pay other people to submit my blog posts to blog carnivals, to do article marketing and other various low-level marketing tasks.

Steph: What are your main methods of marketing your blog?

Yaro: Today it's all about relationships. This is a complex answer, but essentially if you can foster good relationships with all constituents of your blog—your readers, fellow bloggers and writers, then you win.

Marketing is easy when you generate word of mouth. Word of mouth comes from strong brand exposure reinforced by positive relationships.

From a purely tactical point of view when my blog was just getting started my main marketing strategy was guest blogging, blog carnivals, article marketing, blog comments and getting to know other bloggers in my industry so they would write about me.

Steph: Which marketing tactic has surprised you the most in terms of its effectiveness?

Yaro: Email marketing—I'm always blown away by how effective an email newsletter is for driving a lot of traffic to a blog in a very short amount of time.

Steph: What are your quick and short five best tips for blogging?

Yaro:

Write one post per day

Learn something new each day

Make one blogging friend per day

Leave 5 comments on other blogs per day

Submit to one blog carnival per week

Steph: What is the most common pitfall new bloggers generally fall into?

Yaro: Not writing enough content for long enough to get a result and assuming that just writing a few blog posts will get traffic.

I have an article that pretty much sums up the main reason new bloggers have trouble getting going: The 4 Ways of Building Traffic to a Blog and Why Most Bloggers Pick the Wrong Method (**http://www.entrepreneurs-journey.com/808/the-4-ways-of-building-traffic-to-a-blog-and-why-most-bloggers-pick-the-wrong-method/**)

Steph: If you knew what you know now when you first started, what's the one biggest tip you'd give yourself today?

Yaro: I'd tell myself to focus on building an email list from day one and forget about making money for at least six months. Having an email list is critical if you want to launch a real business around your blog.

Steph: What repels you the most from a blog (animations, in your face advertising, etc.)?

Yaro: Poor blog design is something that can definitely hurt, however I think bloggers with nothing original to say is the main reason why I would not go back to a blog. There are so few bloggers who write about unique ideas that those who do garner the lion share of attention.

Steph: Do you make any direct money from your blog through advertising, product placements, etc.?

Yaro: Yes, I make anywhere between $6,000 and $10,000 per month from my blog selling advertising and promoting affiliate products.

Steph: What is your best monetization method (Ads, affiliate marketing, etc.)?

Yaro: My favorite is affiliate marketing, although selling advertising is quite good too. The best way to make money from a blog is to use it to build traffic and establish credibility and then sell your own products and services, since the profits are greater.

Steph: Do you find you get more from direct monetization of your blog or from opportunities that come because of the existence of your blog?

Yaro: Before I launched BlogMastermind.com I got more from direct advertisements on my blog. Once I launched a mentoring program that charges a monthly fee, that became my biggest source of income and it came about because of the fame of my blog.

Steph: What's your most interesting story related to your blog and blogging experience?

Yaro: I'm about to be featured in a movie about bloggers. I'm not entirely sure how it's going to work but it definitely sounds intriguing as the producers are flying around the world to film ten famous bloggers. Definitely not something I thought would happen as a result of blogging.

Steph: What's the one biggest opportunity that came to you because of your blog?

Yaro: As a result of blogging I've got to know a lot of well known people in my industry. Guys who make millions every year.

I'm not the type of person to get star struck, but I do appreciate success and I know how important it is to know successful people.

Without my blog, I would not have the contacts I do.

Steph: Any other comments or thoughts you'd like to share?

Yaro: If you are thinking of starting a blog—go for it. Just remember that it's a slow process and you better enjoy the journey.

If you just do it for the money then don't bother, look for other ways to make money. Blogging is just as much about creative expression and interacting with other people who share your passions, as it is about making money from it.

Good luck!

Epilogue

Although blogging is still a newer medium it's exploding at a phenomenal rate. With 1.4 blogs being created each day according to Technorati.com blogging is definitely a hot topic today. 120,000 new blogs are created each day, the population size of a small city!

And as you've experienced from reading this book, there are many successes. Some bloggers get more unique visitors to their blogs than some major city newspapers, which is incredible when you consider the large sphere of influence these people have. Others are making enough revenues from their blogs to make blogging their career. They earn enough money that their day jobs are constraining their revenues. On the other hand others are using their blogs to bootstrap their services and products, from consulting to many other ventures. It's incredible the success experienced by the bloggers in this book!

If you need any motivation to get started or to keep on blogging, then this book certainly provides it for you. These bloggers have shown you what's possible. But even more importantly, they've shown you how it's possible.

It's not just their knowledge that they've shared with you, they've also given you an incredible amount of references to further enhance your blogging. Take this advice to heart, they know what they're doing, they've all succeeded.

I have to admit that after compiling this book I've never been as motivated as I am today. These people have really inspired me to new heights of success. In between the time that I started the interviews to when I'm writing this epilogue, I've already enhanced my own blog (**FollowSteph.com**) in so many great ways. And I still have so much to do!

If you haven't started blogging yet, what are you waiting for? This book is overflowing at the seams with great information and tips, it has everything you need to start, not to mention all the great references for further detailed information. And if you're already a blogger, I have no doubt you've learned a lot from the interviews, and you're ready to start implementing some of your newfound knowledge.

The biggest tip I can offer you is re-read this book at least one more time. There's a wealth of information in it, more than can be absorbed with one reading. Even now I still find myself learning new things each pass, and I've compiled this book!

Good luck and best successes with your blogging.

Index

Q–R

S

T

U–V

W

Y